CHARISMA IMPROVEMENT

GUIDE TO EFFECTIVE COMMUNICATION IMPROVEMENT TO ENHANCE SELF CONFIDENCE, PUBLIC SPEAKING, AND SOCIAL SKILLS

JOHN WARD

CONTENTS

"How can you have charisma? Be more concerned about making others feel good about themselves than you are making them feel good about you."

--Dan Reiland

THANK YOU!

As a way of saying thank you, I would like to offer you a free copy of my book for free! If you would like to get a copy of it yourself, click the link below! I hope you like it!

CLICK HERE- https://bit.ly/3fuFuni

circumstances is the author responsible for any losses, direct or indirect, that are incurred as a result of the use of the information contained within this document, including, but not limited to, errors, omissions, or inaccuracies.

INTRODUCTION

In 2015, the President of the United States stepped on the podium to address violence.

Before him, a sea of journalists stretched out in a small room. Only specific news corporations and entities were invited, but they each had considerable influence over the general public. The press conference was held to address a rather serious issue: school shootings. Not every reporter in the room was ready to support the president. Some had views that were shared by POTUS, while others held views that could challenge his ideas and decisions.

Regardless of what beliefs the reporters held, the president's job was to unite them all under one banner of thought. That wasn't going to be easy. In fact, if anything, it was an uphill battle.

The president knew that the reporters – and the millions of people watching him on TV – were going to hang on to his every word. A single slip-up, and he might as well have opted to take a long vacation instead of running the office for the second time. Heck, he could have picked up a hobby or completed his "top 100 books to read" list, if he had one. He could be doing a hundred things that did not involve talking to millions of people, and a swarm of reporters.

Instead, president Barack Obama decided to avoid beating around the bush. He dove head-first into the problem, talking about how during previous mass shootings, all the prayers that were offered were not enough. He talked about new changes and a reformed method of handling violence.

Four minutes into the speech, and you could barely hear anyone shuffling in their seats. The room was hanging on to his every word. He had broached a sensitive topic and not one reporter in the room had any complaints about how he had handled the situation.

How did he do it? How could he sway the opinions of so many people and influence them so well?

In fact, think back to the last time you had to handle a rather difficult topic. How was your approach? Did you think that perhaps you should begin with some kindness, hoping to show that you are approaching the listener under a white flag? Or did you crack a joke in an attempt to show just how confident and charismatic you are?

Eventually, you might have realized that your attempt might not have worked. Your joke might have fallen flat or – in most cases – the person might have realized you were only being nice or funny because you wanted something, which might have made things a little awkward.

So what was different with Barack Obama? Was it the fact that he was quite bold in his approach? That's not true. You could be bold, but in certain situations, your boldness might make you look like an ass. In fact, the listener might be thinking about the myriad of ways he would like to rearrange the features on your face.

So what exactly is the secret? That's what you are going to find out as we journey through the world of charisma. We are going to understand what you should do and what you shouldn't in order to be and act charismatic. And let me tell you, it isn't always about trying to imitate Tony Stark. In fact, while we are on the topic of Iron Man himself, let's try and talk about something important.

You have seen Tony Stark when he gets into his suit and dispatches the bad guys with laser beams. And then you have seen him just be funny with his teammates. You have also seen him show genuine sadness and mental anguish. Yet through all of these emotional phases, you always wondered how he could act so charismatic all the time. It is as though the man could talk about the end of the world and the only thought in your mind would be, "Boy does he speak so well. Huh, what? End of the world?"

Being charismatic does not mean you have to cancel your emotional centers and look like you are about to pose for the cover of Vogue. It simply means you understand yourself better and know how to represent yourself in various situations.

Who am I?

I'm your friendly neighborhood charisma teacher. And with my great powers of charismatic knowledge, comes a great responsibility. One where I impart on you the methods, advice, and secrets of charisma. Spoiler alert: it does not matter if you are an introvert or an extrovert. All that matters is how you approach the situation. After all, it isn't about your 'swagger,' as many people would like to put it. It is about your personality, your character, and how well you are in tune with your emotions.

I have been interested in charisma ever since I understood what that word truly meant. When I was in high school, I could define myself in a few words, mainly "gangsta," "cool," or "rad." And none of those words made a modicum of sense. In fact, I wasn't a member of a violent gang of criminals, my core body temperature wasn't that of ice, and I don't even know what rad meant.

But I wanted to improve myself. I once wanted to be like Bruce Lee, quiet and deadly. Until I realized that chopping a wooden board does not always break it, but it could break your hands.

As I grew up, I began to understand more about myself and delve more into psychology, social behavior, and sociology. I began to understand people in general. And when I truly wanted to force myself into a situation where I could interact with people and truly understand human behavior, I took a flight to Bali.

And then one to Turkey, Costa Rica, France, Vietnam, Mexico, South Korea, Japan, Toronto, Ireland, Burssels, and Norway.

Instead of just looking at things from the sidelines, I took a leap of faith without an emotional or psychological parachute. Because of what I did, I began to truly understand what charisma means. I understood what it meant to have genuine human connections, to influence people, to be a magnetic person, and hook people's attention like moths attracted to a flame.

So why wait any further? Let's get started.

HOW COMMUNICATION SKILLS
HELP YOU SUCCEED

A couple of years ago, I was invited to a business conference involving some influential people. Since I was just about to leave work and head over to that conference directly, I didn't have time to change into something befitting the event. However, I wasn't dressed half-bad, if I do say so myself.

Once I arrived at the conference, I noticed that people had already formed groups. Initially, nobody wanted to talk to the rather simple-attired person in their midst. After all, it wasn't as though I was adorned in any ostentatious display of wealth, like some of the other people in the room.

Soon, people began to find out just who was one of the most interesting conversationalists among them (plot twist: it was me). You see, I didn't rely on my physical presentation to grab attention: I used one of the most important aspects of charisma, the art of communication.

However, I would like to point out that I am not going to say that physical presentation is not important. It absolutely is and we are going to discuss why later on.

Conventional forms of advice always begin with what you are supposed to do in order to strengthen communication efforts. However, I am going to start with a few truths on what you should not be doing.

CREATE POSITIVE EXPERIENCES

People don't like communicating with someone who puts them through a bad experience. A lot of the time, people don't care about giving a second chance either.

Here's what I mean. When I first moved to the city I now live in, I was invited to go for a job interview. I was given a set of directions that I followed perfectly. However, when I arrived at the destination, I drove around the block for about 15 minutes. I even used a map application to make sure that I was in the right direction. When I referred to the instructions provided, I knew that I had not made a mistake. I then parked my car and decided to walk around, hoping to have better luck.

Well, I did have better luck. Eventually.

Turns out, the place was located inside an alleyway that would have been difficult to notice if you were driving by.

And here is the kicker. When I entered the alleyway, I had to reach the end of it before realizing that the "company" I was about to visit simply had a door with the number '8' on it. There was nothing else, not even a placard to show that there was an actual business behind the door. For all intents and purposes, I could open the door and enter the den of a deranged cult.

I had a bad experience. Based on that bad experience, I did not have positive interactions with that employer.

In real life, people are sometimes more accepting of certain incidents. They are willing to go past it and give you another chance. But that does not always happen, and finding those specific criteria that determine whether a person is going to have a positive or negative reaction towards you seems like a rather odd idea.

What you should do is try to create a good first

impression. When you decide to take someone out on a date, you don't suggest dumpster diving or plastic collection as your preferred activity. You try to think of something safe – such as a movie, coffee, or dinner – or something unique to that person – such as bowling or visiting an art gallery. You try to create a positive impression. Even when you are getting ready for the date, you don't throw on a towel around your waist and put on last week's t-shirt. You make an attempt to look presentable.

And here is the most important reason to create a positive experience for someone: it shows that you care about them. You have thought about their interests, expectations, mood, and situation. Otherwise, and in certain situations, it might seem as though you don't give a rat's ass about them. In fact, this could be true if you are meeting the person for the first time.

Whether it is in your personal or your professional life, aim to create a positive experience: people will love you for it.

People definitely loved me for it. When I was a recruiter, I always ensured that potential candidates would receive the right information about the job they were applying for. No fluff, no false information, and they could easily glean all the pertinent information about the job. When they would eventually come in for an interview, they would be more confident and have a more positive demeanour. Because of the effort I put into the job descriptions, they had a good first impression of the company.

This positive experience is something that you can achieve in your professional or your personal life. It just takes a little effort.

Creating positive experiences isn't just about adding a fancy job description or setting up your living room so that people who visit your house form a positive impression of you. I have seen people try to explain themselves when the situation demanded no explanations.

What do I mean?

You might have tattoos on your arms. There is a particular shirt you like to wear. You have a unique way of speaking, or you might have an accent. From your facial features that might have a unique combination to it, to the way you present yourself, you are representing yourself. Stop explaining yourself.

When it comes to communication, explaining yourself creates the impression that you are insecure about your traits or not confident about them.

If someone asks you about your characteristics, style, or appearance choices, you don't have to feel nervous and start giving your life story. For example, let's say you have a tattoo on your neck. If you were presented with a question about that tattoo, give a brief, but polite response. Sometimes, you might be presented with a few more questions. In such cases, answer them only if you want to. You don't have to feel compelled to explain, especially if the person is a stranger. There is no need to justify something that holds meaning to you. I would go so far as to say that you don't have to justify anything. You don't need someone else's approval to be who you are.

I do realize that real life situations are far more complex, and do not follow a binary set of rules. However, when you learn to not explain yourself for trivial reasons – or when it is not necessary – then you will understand when an explanation is truly required.

I'm going to go in-depth into being comfortable in your own skin in a later chapter. For now, remember that the more you try to explain something, the more you end up looking like you are guilty of something. And that diminishes the positive impression you are trying to establish.

This is true even when you don't have all the information. I see people say too much or provide too many explanations when they don't have all the information. Sometimes, they do it because they want to look smarter, or have this idea that a lack of knowledge makes them look stupid.

Do you know why many people love stand-up comedians? Because they have a sense of genuine character about them. But have you ever wondered why that is?

Here is the trick: they don't pretend to know everything.

They make fun of the things that they do know. People enjoy the experiences and unique perspectives of stand-up comedians. We always think of them as smart, witty, clever, and fun, not because they could tell you the atomic number of tungsten, but because they double-down on their skills.

In today's world, common forms of wisdom following the vein of the below statements:

- Fake it till you make it!
- If you want to be successful, act successful!

But real life is not that simple.

In today's world, people are more aware and knowledgeable than before, thanks to the expanding power of the internet. You may think that you can pretend to be something, but when people find out that you don't, your credibility is going to drop, and with it the image you have built in the minds of people.

When you come forth as a know-it-all, people find it grating. Additionally, it takes away any semblance of genuineness that the conversation holds. Don't worry about trying to prove that you are smart because the truth is, people remember someone who is interesting more than they recall someone who is smart.

Try to remember this; a positive experience does not happen simply because you know more facts than the average person. It happens because of your character and personality.

You create a positive experience with the way you speak, the way you present yourself, and how you treat the other person. I know that 'stewardesses' is the longest word that you can type on your keyboard using only your left hand. That's a cool fact isn't it? I mean, you might be impressed right now. But just because I impressed you, does that mean that I created a positive experience for you? Forget the fact that you have been reading this book and you know me a little by now. If you happened to meet me for the first time and I was trying too hard to show that I am smart, would you find me charming?

Would I have created a positive experience for you? Or would you think I was arrogant, or a show-off?

Positive experiences come from you. It is about how you treat others and how you reveal to them what kind of a person you are. And you should focus on being genuine.

Another important aspect of creating positivity is to avoid using a categorical statement, a statement that places an assertion or rejection of an entire claim, as it does not present itself as genuine. You know what you said isn't true, and the other person knows it as well.

For example, a friend of mine recently got into an argument with a colleague. The person on the other end of the argument claimed that she would never do 'anything' to delay someone's work. Whether the claim was true or not, it came off as not genuine.

Other examples of a categorical statement using the 'always' clause:

- I have always been honest with you.
- I have always made sure that I was there to listen to you.

Remember this: nothing is 100%. When you use

statements that include the 'always' or 'never' clause, you are asserting that there has not been a single moment when you deviated from the claim you made.

It is okay to admit imperfections. After all, it makes you human. People like talking to someone who has human characteristics.

Keep in mind that you are trying to create a positive experience for others. And to do so, you have to bring out the positivity from within you.

Now I can make a guess on what you are thinking right now. Perhaps you are thinking that you are not a negative person. In fact, your nickname might as well be Positive Positivity McPositiveness. Creating a positive experience might be easy!

But what I am talking about is not about always being happy or joyful. I am not talking about avoiding rudeness. I am talking about positivity in communication, and that has a whole new meaning.

So what exactly do I mean by "positive"?

- Adopt a sense of empathy. Try to genuinely understand what the person is trying to convey. Just because the person provided a contradictory statement, it does not mean that he or she is wrong, or that he or she is trying to start a fight. Maybe they just want to express themselves.

- Be sensitive about the topic, if required. For example, if you have broached the topic of mental health issues, then don't throw a joke in there because you want to show how funny you are.

- Positivity is not about looking at "the bright side" of things. It is a culmination of various characteristics, such as humility, empathy, kindness, and carefulness, where you are careful about the words you employ and of course, avoid ad hominems. In fact, the best way to understand the concept of positivity in communication is to think of as avoiding negative traits such as garbled messaging, inaccurate information, use of the wrong emotion, and other such factors that affect the message you want to convey.

BECOME STRONGER

By growing stronger, I don't mean that you have to build muscles that deflect bullets. What I mean is that you need to add more strength to your communication or messages.

I have heard people mention that one should be assertive when they communicate, but they don't mention how.

There are a few things you can do to strengthen your character and communication, starting with trying to not diffuse tension when you face it.

I was once in a meeting with important people from a partner company.

During the meeting, everyone got a chance to speak up and present their ideas. Most of the participants in the meeting used loud and exaggerated actions to present their ideas. When my turn came, I didn't put up an act. I use a calm and confident manner to get to the point. When it was time to be funny, I used a few jokes here and there, nothing big, and no joke so funny that I wanted the person to fall over laughing. After all, my goal was not the jokes, but the content of the presentation.

One of the members of the partner company, who was a top brass and also a multi-millionaire, looked at me when I sat down and made a comment about my work.

"Why weren't you like the others? Be bold. Don't be a p@%#*, man," said the multi-millionaire.

Now most people would feign a laugh or chuckle to themselves in order to diffuse the situation. I wasn't about to take a comment like that in its stride. I looked at the multi-millionaire straight in the eye, and using a measured tone I said, "Don't call me a p@%#*."

For a while, nobody said anything. Eventually, the multi-millionaire said, "My bad. I didn't mean to offend you."

You are an individual with value. Don't let anyone talk down on you. When you know that you are not in the wrong, firmly, but calmly, reject the offense thrown at you. Show strength in your communication through confidence.

Speaking of confidence; practice it.

It is easier said than done. But most people confuse confidence with bravado. When I use the word confidence, I am asking you to be sure of yourself, and not be a d*@#.

But how can one be sure of themselves without appearing arrogant? Well, simplicity is the key, I say.

That sounds like a vague statement. What does it mean to maintain simplicity? How about looking at the opposite? Don't exaggerate.

When you have a message to communicate, use the simplest language to get your point across. The more you try to add explanations, the more unsure you will sound. Get to the point.

But even getting to the point presents its own set of challenges. After all, you might not be certain if you are going to get the results you want. You might think that by getting to the point quickly, you are going to create such an impression, that the listener will have to believe you, accept your proposal, or do what you want them to do. Reality however, is quite different. My recommendation to you would be to expect the unexpected.

This might be a difficult idea to hold on to, but make sure that you don't unrealistically expect positive responses to your messages or requests. What do I mean by that?

Let's say you are about to ask for a week's leave from work to your boss. You probably know your boss is fairly stern and strict at the office. When communicating, your role is to send across the message clearly. If it is absolutely required that you add an explanation in order to provide a reason for your request, then do so in a concise manner. Don't – as the saying goes – "beat around the bush." Your responsibility is to make sure that you get your point across well. At the same time, know that your boss could either accept or reject your request. You cannot predict the outcome and you cannot control the other person. So don't enter a conversation with the idea that there is only one fixed conclusion.

Keep this rule in mind, for communication and for practically everything else in life: you can expect the best, but always prepare for the worst.

One of the best ways to differentiate between the best and the worst possibilities is to understand what you are supposed to do. How do you help sail the boat? How are you keeping consistent with someone's vision? What is your role? In most casual situations where you are just talking to people without trying to achieve anything, you don't have to worry about goals. After all, your only goal is to have an engaging conversation. But in a professional situation, it is important to know what your role and goals are. It helps you understand what is the best outcome you can achieve, and what is the worst.

Our minds are pretty complex structures. They are capable of latching on to an idea, and they are equally capable of meandering between different ideas and thoughts. Don't let your mind move around too much. Keep it focused on the message at hand.

Before you even begin to communicate, fix the communication goal you want to achieve.

- Are you requesting something?
- Do you need information?
- Would you like to receive a clarification?

Whatever your goal is, don't lose sight of it.

Remember that whether the situation is heading towards the best outcome, or the worst, stick to presenting facts and information.

Do not attack a person. In other words, avoid Ad Hominems.

Just scroll through comment sections on YouTube and you might see 60% of hate-filled, aggressive, insulting, and derogatory comments and just 40% of responses filled with logic and reasoning.

Don't be part of the group that reacts and targets a person. Be in the reason and logic camp.

The term "ad hominem" is short for "argumentum ad hominem" and it refers to an argument that is directed at an individual rather than the content or logic of that individual. In other words, it is a cheap shot. People use ad hominem when they realize they are about to be proven wrong or they don't have enough logic to support their arguments. By attacking a person, they want him or her to react emotionally, thereby placing that person in a bad light.

Most of the time, people who use ad hominem arguments are not confident about themselves or their logic. Don't attack the person. Stick to your guns.

But what if you are wrong? What if the logic that you are trying to apply is not the right one?

Then admit you are wrong. It is as simple as that.

When you admit that your viewpoint was wrong, there are a few things that are going to happen:

- You become a better person. Admitting you are wrong does not mean you are weak or stupid. It just means you are an individual who has the confidence to learn.
- You gain credibility. People will realize that you are the kind of person who admits when they are wrong. Which means that in the future, you won't believe that something is right if you are not too sure of yourself.
- Finally, you learn something.

AS A LEADER, COMMUNICATION IS IMPORTANT

When you are leading a team, you should leave no room for uncertainty. You cannot be vague or unintelligible. There cannot be room for ambiguity. Your messaging and instructions should be concrete.

When you are a leader, you are the captain of the ship. Whether you are going to take your crew on a journey of growth and success, or crash into an iceberg and sink, is entirely up to you.

With proper communication, you can point your crew in the right direction. You are able to tell them where you want to go. You have a goal, which helps you in two important ways:

- You attract the kind of crew who are willing to travel with you all the way. They know what they are getting into, and they are happy to come on board.
- You clearly communicate what each crew member is supposed to do. Additionally, you also understand just how many people you need to get you to your destination. In other words, you

hire the right kind of people, and the
right number of people.

Over the course of my career, I have managed
numerous teams, some of them over 80 people
strong. Despite the large numbers, I was able to
achieve the goals set forth by the organization and
ensure people were able to work well with each
other.

How did I do that? Simple. I learned how to
communicate.

I'm not talking about wearing a suit and walking
into my department as if I am the "Wolf of Wall
Street" - not even close. I understood that it is important to be open, clear, respectful, and confident.

It is vital that your message is received in a
manner that is exactly or as close as possible to your
intended meaning. In order to avoid misunderstandings, you need to be able to bring together the ideas
in your head into a 'streamlined' message, a message
that gets your point across without adding too many
unnecessary details. You might think this is easy.
Many people think it's quite instinctive to be able to
speak what's on your mind properly. In reality
however, things are not that easy. We might say one
thing, but the person might misconstrue the meaning

of our words, and that does not bode well for the relationship we have established with the other person.

Most of what you express is a form of communication. The smile you offer, the joke you share, even the amount of time you spend listening to the other person are all ways you communicate.

If your communication fails, you can create misunderstandings, and those misunderstandings are only going to damage the relationships you might have taken a long time to establish.

Try to listen more than you speak. You are not in a race. In fact, you can provide a proper response or a compelling argument if you listen to the other person carefully.

When you experience a moment of silence, don't feel compelled to speak.

In the early 1980s, a famous astronomer said in one of the episodes of his television series that we are made of star stuff. Yes, I am talking about Carl Sagan. Millions of people around the world have been entranced by the words of the astrophysicist and cosmologist. Even now, people listen to his lecture and can't help but feel a profound sensation of being transported to another space and time.

But why was Carl Sagan able to gather so much interest? Was it because he was so smart and knowledgeable? Hardly. You can find videos where his speech has been superimposed on an assortment of stock videos, and it still sounds engaging.

Carl Sagan was a splendid orator because he managed his pauses. He wasn't afraid of them nor did he feel compelled to add anything to cover them. This is true for practically anyone who is capable of giving an incredible speech or commanding the audience. From Larry King to Ursula K. Le Guin, the famous American author, you can see how people have learned to use silence to their advantage.

If you find yourself facing silence, don't pay attention to the situation, but think about what you would like to say next. If nothing comes to mind, then don't feel compelled to pitch in. Remember that the responsibility of adding something to the conversation does not solely lie with you.

Let the other person speak. And if they can't, move on. Do something else. Seriously, don't stand or sit there looking awkward.

However, when you are presented with an opportunity to speak, then make a boom!

What do I mean?

I remember this one evening, after a long day at work, I ended up proclaiming "I am so tired, I look like a dead person walking." My colleagues smiled. Some chuckled.

Around 30 minutes later, my colleague Tom walked in and boisterously said, "Holy s&#t! I feel like a zombie!" People laughed.

I began to wonder why. What was the difference in the joke that Tom and I just said? Nothing. In fact, mine was more creative and less vulgar. I deserved the praise more than Tom did. But I began to wonder again: my ego got the better of me. Of course Tom received a better response. Because Tom didn't care.

I was trying so hard to get a response that I forgot that the most important aspect about a joke is the delivery. It is why stand-up comedians are good at what they do. They know how to tell a joke.

It does not matter whether you are trying to be funny or telling something informative. What matters is that you make an impact each time you do. If you don't get the right response, move on. Don't get hung up over it and allow it to give you a sense of defeat.

Be confident in what you have to say. After all, you cannot confidently predict what the other person is going to say or react, so focus on yourself.

When I was younger, I loved talking about movies. Every time I used to talk about a good movie,

I would say, "Guys, this movie is pretty good." There was a rise in pitch on one word while another barely sounded audible. Pretty soon, I learnt to make a statement, and I would confidently say, "Guys, this movie is good. I recommend it."

When making a statement, do it confidently. It does not mean that you are ignoring everyone else's requests or talking down to them. It simply means that you are giving your perspective on things.

Take Tom for example (the same Tom I talked about a few paragraphs ago). He was like that: the best thing about him was that he would make a statement, but when someone else provided a better solution, he would never hesitate to admit that the other person was right. In fact, he would make another statement, such as, "That's not a bad idea. Let's do it!" Not only did he show a sense of humility, but he showed that he could make a statement even though he was not in the right.

ON HAVING AN ISSUE

I know that sometimes, people have genuine personality or mental health issues: in such cases, one cannot simply tell them to change their attitude and become confident.

If you have a personality or mental health issues, then I urge you to seek help.

Why?

Because I don't think it is fair that you should be deprived of being your best self, or contributing something, or simply making the most out of what this world has to offer. You deserve to chase your dreams, jump off a plane (with a parachute of course), binge-watch Netflix documentaries, or swoon over Henry Cavill's perfectly chiselled face / be hypnotized by Ana de Armas's alluring beauty.

I honestly believe that you deserve all the opportunities that come your way and if something is stopping you from grabbing those opportunities, then you should try and deal with that blockage. A close friend of mine battled with depression for a long time. It was only due to his therapist and the support of his family and friends, that he was able to make great improvements in his condition. Now I am not saying that he suddenly became so charming that he was able to gather world leaders and convince them they should try to achieve world peace; however, he was able to confidently deal with social situations, say no unflinchingly (which trust me, was extremely difficult for him), and stand up for his beliefs.

Don't think you have no hope. You do.

2

BECOME A LISTENER

I am a decent cook. My skills are not at par with Gordon Ramsay's, but I make a mean pasta.

Once I found myself talking to my barber about pasta. The guy talked about how he prepared it using his mother's recipe. He believed that you need to have enough salt in the water, or the pasta is not going to taste good. According to him, you need to have at least a tablespoon of salt for every 3 liters of water. I was skeptical about his recommendation, but I didn't show my skepticism. Instead, I genuinely engaged with him about his pasta-making skills, allowing him to speak most of the time and only interjecting when I didn't understand something.

That night, I decided to try out his recipe. And lo

and behold, the man was right. The pasta tasted so much better.

To think I got this tip from a barber.

Just because you are good at something, it does not mean that you don't listen to others.

Listening is important. But there is more to it than getting a recipe for pasta.

When you genuinely listen, you can use the right information to create your message. The other person in turn responds to your message, and so on and so forth. If you cut someone off, you are only using a part of the information to create a message, which only makes your job more difficult, since now you have to find ways to seek the missing information and rearrange your message to accommodate the new information.

At the same time, listening properly might just help you reach goals faster. Even though you have to spend an hour or more communicating with someone because you were listening to them talk, it is far better than interrupting them. When you don't listen properly, then you are going to operate under incomplete information.

My ex-colleague Sarah had a bad habit of cutting in when people were talking. In one of the meetings with the team leader – where we were all receiving a new set of tasks – she cut him midway as he was explaining her responsibilities. She assumed that she knew what the leader was talking about.

Here's what happened. When she eventually completed the task in a record two days time (which was an incredible result at that time, given the task), she realized that she had skipped one tiny detail. Truly, it was as tiny as "take this number and make sure it is kept here." It took another three days for her to fix the problem and redo the work.

If only she had taken the time to listen properly, then she would have completed the work on time. This is true in your life. Don't interrupt the flow of information. Listen. And listen some more.

Let us look at a way to improve listening skills.

Here is a task that you can do when you get the time.

Call up a close friend or family member (or anyone you can talk to comfortably) and then do the following.

1. Pick up a topic that they are interested in and allow them to talk. It would be preferable if you pick a topic you know nothing about.

2. Now listen to them explain the topic. Do

not interrupt them. If you have any
questions, then make a mental note of
them.

3. When the person completes explaining,
   then ask your questions. For each
   question you ask, make sure that you
   listen to the other person entirely.

4. Once you have completed getting all the
   information, write down or, to make
   things more simpler, create an audio
   recording highlighting everything you
   have learned so far.

Once you have completed the task, gauge yourself using the below questions.

- How well did you listen to the person?
- Were you able to remember asking all
  the questions you wanted to ask?
- Were you able to recollect the
  information properly?

Now rate your level of understanding on the
scale provided below:

- 5 Stars- I could understand the concept

really well. Call me the 'sensei' of the
topic.

- 4 Stars- I understood most of what was
said.
- 3 Stars- I understood some of the
meaning of the topic.
- 2 Stars- I barely understood what had
been said to me. Was that even English?
- 1 Star- Who? What? When? Where?

Next, rate your level of recall using the scale
provided below:

- 5 Stars-You can call me The
Supercomputer.
- 4 Stars- Not bad. I am impressed with
how much I could recall.
- 3 Stars- I could remember some of what
was being said.
- 2 Stars- I can remember the beginning
and the end.
- 1 Star- Who? What? When? Where?

*D*on't allow the score to disappoint you. Unless of course, you got the highest score, in which case you probably won't be disappointed. The reason you shouldn't feel down about the score is because there are ways you can improve it by using the exercise given below.

We are going to watch a movie. Or a television series.

Here is how the exercise works.

1. Take three minutes of your favorite movie or television series, preferably one that has a combination of dialogue and action.
2. Now watch the scene. Do not pay attention to anything else except what is happening on the screen.
3. Take a piece of paper (or use a recording device) and describe in as much detail as possible what happens in the scene.
4. Watch the scene again.
5. Describe the scene again, this time adding in details that you had missed on your first viewing of the scene.
6. Repeat the above two steps to add in

details that you might have missed on your second viewing.

Repeat the above exercise every day, but make sure that you use a different scene for each exercise. Once you begin to get comfortable with recollecting scenes that are three minutes long, extend the view time to five minutes, then go for seven minutes, and so on.

Do not think about how quickly or slowly your powers of recollection improve. The most important point is that you are improving.

Here is a variation:

1. Pick your favorite book. It does not matter if the book is a work of fiction or not. Turn to any page of the book and then read the page slowly. There is no time limit, so don't be in a rush.

2. Once you have completed reading the page, take another piece of paper (or recorder) and then recollect the contents of what you read as they appeared on the page.

3. Do not rearrange the information. If you cannot recollect a part of the page, then

move on to the next part. Your main goal is to organize the parts as much as possible.

4. Now go through the page again and then arrange the information, this time adding in the details that you had originally missed out.

5. Repeat the exercise a third time.

Continue practicing this exercise, increasing the number of pages to two and then eventually three when you get used to working with a single page.

You should also focus on your comprehension skills.

You can improve your ability to understand something through a simple exercise. Here is what you should do.

Pick a topic. Any topic. Here are some suggestions:

- Gold Mining
- Tectonic Plates
- American History
- Animal Behavior

Find and read an article about your chosen topic, then follow these steps:

Step 1: Ask Questions

Start asking more questions about your chosen topic.

- Why does this happen?
- What would be the result if the opposite happened?
- What is the purpose or goal of this?
- If there is no detailed information about this topic, why is that?
- Did I understand everything about the topic? If not, why? Should I find more information?

Step 2: Explain The Idea

In this step, take all the information that you have and present it to an invisible audience. Think of the best way to bring all the information together. Ideally, try to explain it using analogies and metaphors, if possible.

Step 3: Look For Additional Information

Once you are able to explain the topic fairly well, look for additional information to strengthen the knowledge that you already have. You don't have to look for too much additional information. You just have to look for enough to support the knowledge that you already have.

Step 4: Explain The Idea... Again

This time, with the new information that you have collected. Once again, try to use analogies and metaphors. Keep your explanations as simple as possible.

Once you have completed the previous exercise, move on to the next exercise. In this exercise, pick up any philosophical topic and then follow the below steps:

Step 1: Explain What It Means (In Your Own Words)

There is no right or wrong answer. Just explain to yourself what you understand about the topic.

Step 2: Support It

Next, try to bring up arguments to support the statement. You can even take this moment to perform your own research into the subject if you like. Remember, do not take into consideration any ideas or information that oppose it. Only focus on the information that supports your viewpoint on the subject.

Step 3: Now Oppose It

In this step, find out the reason to oppose your

viewpoint. Lay down all the statements you have made to support your viewpoint on a piece of paper. Then go online and find out as much information as you can to oppose it. You are technically going against yourself, but the point is to create a compelling argument to easily oppose your viewpoint (and come out as a winner), or be able to provide enough reasons to explain your opposing views clearly.

People think that listening is all about keeping quiet and allowing the other person to speak. It is not. Anybody can shut up and listen, it's not a difficult skill to master.

What you have to do is listen responsively.

When you listen responsively, you are putting into practice three vital characteristics:

- Comprehension
- Evaluation
- Retention

By simply listening, you are doing, well, none of the above. You are not comprehending what the person is saying; you are just showing what a good listener you are. If you cannot comprehend, then what is there to evaluate? You might as well jump to a conclusion. And let's not even go into retention because why does it even matter at this point?

If comprehension is like running a 100 meter relay, retention is like going through a marathon. If you are not going to do the former, then don't even bother with the latter.

The exercises mentioned earlier help you train the aforementioned three characteristics.

THE ART OF LISTENING

Once you have trained yourself to truly listen to somebody, there are a few things that you can do to enhance your listening skills.

Face the speaker. This is important because too often, people become distracted by things going on around them. You are listening to someone. You aren't listening to your phone or the walls.

Eye contact is one of the most important criteria for listening properly. If you are uncomfortable looking at someone in the eyes, then try to look at the space between the eyes. If you are the one to speak, then make eye contact before saying something, not after.

Your entire body should be facing the person, especially the shoes. Oh yes, the angle of your shoes matter. Here's a tip; do you want to know if someone is interested in you or not in a social situation? Then look at their shoes. If their body is pointed towards you but their feet are angling away from you, then they just want to get the hell out of there.

Regardless of how they respond to you, don't worry too much about it. Don't allow your head to focus on the other person. Bring it back to yourself. Relax.

Now that you have made eye contact, hold it for at least four or five seconds. Make sure that you are relaxed. You don't have to look like you are about to get reprimanded for something.

When you are tense, then the speaker subconsciously latches onto the tension you are projecting. He or she then becomes uncomfortable, reserved, apprehensive, doubtful, or skeptical. They simply don't want to communicate honestly.

Relax, whether you are standing or sitting. Additionally, once you have made eye contact for a few seconds, feel free to look away from time to time. You don't have to stare at people like you are going to devour them with a side of mashed potatoes and red wine.

If you want to look away, look to the sides, rather than looking down.

It is important to keep your mind empty. When I say empty, I mean that you should remove any semblance of biases, prejudices, or any feelings you have about the person or the topic of interest. Ease into the topic with an open mind. Without preconditioned notions or ideas, you will be able to genuinely listen to what the other pays says or does. Some people listen only because they are waiting to say what's on their mind. It could be a truly funny joke that they think could make them the next Dave Chappelle, or an interesting fact so ingenious, Neil deGrasse Tyson might want to invite them over for a beer.

But do not listen because you want to speak. Listen because you want to listen. Nod your head. Respond with supporting comments. Try to give feedback to the speaker. I am not saying that you have to constantly nod your head, even when it is not required. But show that you are still listening to the person.

3

GET COMFORTABLE

*T*ry to watch a lawyer present a case and you will notice that he or she might speak extemporaneously, which is a way of speaking that does not sound like it had any preparation.

In reality however, lawyers are always prepared. In fact, they cannot go into the courtroom without preparing their notes.

Despite how much lawyers prepare beforehand, they don't try to speak from their notes verbatim. But what allows them to speak in such a manner? What's the secret of their technique?

Have you heard of the phrase "to become comfortable in your own skin"? That's what lawyers do. They become comfortable in their own skin.

That is our mission in this section; to find out how to become comfortable with ourselves.

And one of the biggest obstacles to being comfortable with yourself is indecision.

Indecision is a difficult habit to get rid of. When you are indecisive, you end up worrying and fearing trivial things because you can't seem to come to a conclusion. Is there something wrong with you? Why is it taking you so much time to make a decision?

I understand that it is not easy to make a decision, especially when both choices you have are equally beneficial to you. However, research has shown that the more time you spend making a decision, the more difficult it may seem.

One of the worst aspects of indecision is that it creates doubts, self-conflicts, and uncertainties. At the same time, it zap your confidence, cripples your flow, and then makes you uncomfortable with yourself. Sometimes, you may start out confident but the longer you are unable to arrive at a decision, then more confidence you strip away.

Here is how to curb indecision.

- Take a breather. Pause your thoughts

and relax. Take a couple or few minutes away from your thoughts.

- Pay attention to your emotions. Are you feeling angry? Sad? Disappointed? Ask yourself if you are truly in the right frame of mind to make a decision. If not, come back to the problem later.

- Think logically. Ask yourself questions. What purpose is this going to serve? What are the benefits? Is it really important that I have to make a specific choice or can I simply choose anything randomly?

Indecision can also happen when you feel that you are lacking something. Quite often, we tend to be quite critical about our physical appearance. We think that just because we don't look a certain way or meet certain beauty standards, we cannot become comfortable with ourselves.

There are some physical flaws that can be treated, while there are others that cannot be dealt with.

But the word 'flaw' is quite a misnomer. You see, it wasn't you who thought of your physical appearance as a flaw. When you were a child, you thought you were normal. It's only when someone pointed it out to you – usually in an insulting, scathing, or derogatory manner – that you realized you had something that was not normal. So who decides what is a flaw and what isn't? Is there a guidebook that people should refer to? If so, to what degree can one consider their appearance as a flaw?

For example, if a person has a crooked nose, then how crooked should it be to be considered a flaw? What should be the ideal angle of the nose? What are acceptable measurements?

Nobody can give you the right answer. That is because nobody knows how accurately to describe a flaw.

Not everyone around the world can look the same. So own your flaws. Don't let them bring you down. Allow yourself to challenge the perceptions made about your appearance. Think for yourself what is the right way to think about your own appearance, don't allow others to decide what you should believe about yourself.

I would also recommend spending more time with yourself to improve your image of yourself.

What do you like doing? Watching Netflix? Playing the guitar? Beating the boss of that really difficult level in your favorite video game?

What gives you a sense of accomplishment? Whatever it is, do it. From cooking to pottery to collecting rocks (hey, I'm not judging), you need to engage in activities that give you a sense of purpose or allow you to feel like you have accomplished something.

When you feel like you got something done, you gain a little more confidence in yourself. That becomes a feedback loop; you gain confidence, you do the activity again, you feel even more confident, and on and on. Eventually, you reach a point where you feel like an absolute badass.

You also start becoming comfortable being alone.

But let me make this clear; being alone does not mean being lonely. They are two different concepts. When you are alone, you are by yourself. However, when you are lonely, you live a solitary existence.

By being alone, you get to understand various aspects about yourself. Just to be clear, I am not saying that you should force yourself to be in a situation where you are alone. When you find yourself in the absence of company, do not attempt to seek it out. Enjoy doing the things that you do.

GETTING COMFORTABLE: MANAGING STRESS

I'm going to start this section by pointing out something important about communication. Don't you hate it when you are sitting across a person and trying to tell them something, but their attention is stuck to a small device in their hands? It gets rather frustrating since you are unsure whether the person is listening to you or does not care about what you have to say.

When you take out your phone, then it shows that you are easily distracted and are not comfortable holding a proper conversation. People who are confident about themselves and their ability to manage a conversation do not have to get distracted easily.

Before you even start a conversation with someone, remove all distractions out of the way. This could be done by an action as simple as keeping your phone on the surface in front of you or turning it to silent mode and placing it in your pocket. Or it could be something more effective as heading over to a quieter place for a conversation or telling everyone to keep their mobile devices in one place until the end of the conversation.

But why did I bring up the topic of keeping your

phones away. For one, you can actually avoid a lot of awkwardness and stress by simply allowing yourself to focus on the conversation, rather than being distracted by anything else.

Now that we have gotten that out of the way, let's talk about the important stuff.

Do you know the trick to managing your stress? First of all, recognize that it is happening to you. Look out for not just mental signs, but physical ones as well.

Do you feel your stomach muscles tightening? Are your hands clenched? Is your breathing shallow? Or do you find yourself holding your breath at certain times?

If your answer is yes to any or all of the above questions, then it means that you are getting stressed. There are two types of stressful situations, those that you should deal with and those that you don't need to deal with immediately.

If you have no other choice other than to deal with the situation:

- Stay calm. Don't get rattled by what the other person said or did. Think about why you are there in the first place.
- Think of ways to buy some time. For

example, you could ask the person to repeat the question again. You could even say, "that's a good question" and start by talking about things that you know. When you begin with information you are familiar with, then you can ease yourself into unfamiliar territory. Alternatively, you can throw the ball in the other person's court by asking for clarification on the question. You don't have to make your clarifications complicated or over-the-top polite. Use the below phrases if you are at a loss for words:

- I'm sorry but I didn't catch what you just said. Could you repeat it again?
- I'm sorry but I didn't understand your question/statement. Could you explain it a little?
- Am I right in thinking that what you meant to say was (insert your understanding)? Please feel free to correct me.
- Could you tell me a bit more of your train of thought? I would like to understand it a bit more.

- Sorry, but I don't quite follow you.
- Remember, be the boss of silence. Don't let it make you nervous. Embrace its power. Use that time to collect your thoughts.
- Make a point quickly and provide one or a few supporting information. If you stick to one point for too long, then you start exaggerating or worse, boring the audience. Get to the point and keep your language simple. For example, don't "extrapolate or disseminate particulars and statistics lucidly". That's just a confusing statement. Just "give the facts clearly".
- If you want to add a summary, then do so quickly. Once you have provided your message, information, or summary, then stop. Don't worry about the silence. You have done your job. There is nothing else for you to do.

On the other hand, if you don't have to continue the conversation, then calmly try to think whether it would be better if you postponed it. This provides you with enough time to bring your stress levels under control and prepare yourself better.

If you find yourself needing to manage your stress in an emergency, then remember these tips.

- Pop a peppermint into your mouth before you start the conversation, interview, or meeting. When you find yourself facing a stressful question or response, then pretend to think about the question or statement while tasting the candy. You can even use a stress ball placed in your pocket or an object to fiddle with, as long it is not noisy, distracting, or obvious.
- Try to find the humor in the situation. When things get too stressful, read the room and try to find out whether humor would be appropriate. If it is, then apply it. Not only will you be able to relieve some of the tension you have been holding on to, but you will help others relax as well.
- If you and the other person seem unable to come to a reasonable conclusion, then you can agree to disagree, whereby each

person tolerates the viewpoint of the other without agreeing to them. This solution can be used to avoid the stressful situation from going out of control.

- Take a deep breath and think before you speak. Often, stress causes us to react instinctively. If you find yourself yearning to say something, stop and think about your response or message. Is it appropriate? Does it target an individual? Do I really want to say that?

Sometimes, when you cannot bring down the stress levels, breathing helps. But most people start taking quick breaths in order to calm themselves.

- If you ever find yourself in a stressful situation, then take a quick break to employ the breathing technique below.
- Draw in a deep breath through your nose, while keeping your mouth clamped firmly shut. Allow this breath to fill up your chest. Feel your chest expand.
- Hold the breath in for a few seconds, then exhale through the mouth.
- Do this a couple of times. After that,

inhale and feel the air fill up your
abdomen. Allow the air to remain there
for a few seconds before exhaling it.
Perform this exercise a couple of times.

As we look at the many ways to get comfortable,
we should also not forget our body language.

If you think that words are the only important
aspect of communication, then you have barely
touched the surface of communication.

Let me tell you about the time I had traveled to
Thailand and witnessed a Muay Thai match. Boy, it
was pretty intense. I don't like combat sports. I prefer a
nice game of baseball with a beer in my hands and the
option to switch to Netflix during commercials. But
when I witnessed Muay Thai, I just saw two people
with so much physical prowess, that it made me want
to go back home, learn the popular martial art, and
maybe even become a Muay Thai-based crime fighter.

When I asked my travel partner more about the
sport, he explained to me how one of the most – if
not THE most – important principle of Muay Thai
is that you use your entire body. You don't use your
legs to do a rope-a-dope; you use them to deliver a
vicious kick so painful that the victim's ancestors will

be able to feel it. Your entire body becomes fluid and dynamic.

When I realized what the principle about Muay Thai was, I recognized a single idea: it shared many aspects with communication. In fact, I would even go so far as to say that Muay Thai is a form of communication. Well, maybe the martial art only sends out messages of aggression, but its comparison to the process of communication is undeniable. Just like Muay Thai, you are using your entire body to send across a message.

If your friend tells you that he or she had a really bad day and your response is to say "I understand," while looking bored, then you are not communicating the right level of sympathy.

One of the important aspects of body language is your posture.

Computers have given us tons of benefits. Except for our posture.

Spending a lot of time at the computer, we gain a hunch, which in turn affects the way we present ourselves to other people. In other words, we appear as though we are not confident. A hunch, or a slumped figure, is a sign of indecision and weakness. Even if you are not the kind of person to be indecisive, your posture will present that problem to viewers.

Let us look at how you can improve your posture.

POSTURE REVIEW

- I would like you to find a full-length mirror. Then try and wear clothing that is not too loose or baggy. Now I would like you to close your eyes and then shake yourself. Just relieve as much of the tension that you have in your body.
- Keep your eyes closed and relax. Don't think about anything or worry about your posture. At least not yet. Now open your eyes and then check out your posture.
- What do you notice? Does your chest look like it has positioned itself inward? Does your bottom look like it is sticking out (and no, that is not a good thing)?
- Now hold a pen in each of your hands (or hold an elongated object like a spoon). Are the pens parallel to each other or are they pointing inwards? If they are

angling towards your body, then your
shoulders are folding inwards.

POSTURE CORRECTION EXERCISE

- Bring your hands behind your back and
  then clasp your fingers. If you can't seem
  to bring your hands together, bring them
  as close to each other as possible and lock
  that position by grabbing a towel or a
  shirt.
- Adjust your body so that your spine,
  neck, and head are all aligned in a
  straight line. Make sure that you are
  looking straight in front of you.
- Now lift your chest up as you bring your
  hands down towards the floor. Start
  taking deep breaths. Hold this position
  for 5 deep breaths.
- Relax your position and then breath
  deeply for 10 breaths.

Repeat the above exercise daily, especially if you
find yourself sitting for most of the day.

When maintaining your posture, also remember

to uncross your arms. People respond to even the most subtle actions. You might think that they are not paying any attention, but in reality, they definitely are. In some cases, people are consciously aware that you don't look confident while in others, they are unconsciously making connections, such as when you cross your arms. Crossing your arms is a defensive maneuver. It shows that you are ready to deflect something or that you are not confident accepting what is being said to you. Additionally, it changes people's stances towards you in the following ways:

- Some of them might become too cautious around you. They feel as though they are walking on eggshells in order to prevent saying something to offend you. When people are too cautious, then it becomes an exhausting exercise for them. Eventually, they start being honest with you.
- In some cases, especially when you are in a meeting with someone important (such as a potential business partner, your boss, or even a colleague), crossing your arms becomes a sign of weakness. Once

someone realizes what buttons to push in order to get you into a defensive stance, they can use it against you just because they can.

When you uncross your arms, you become more open and dynamic. You allow yourself to express your message in numerous ways. There is a sense of "free flow" to your body. It makes you look comfortable and looking at you, people begin to feel comfortable.

Don't communicate with just words, use your body.

- Use gesticulations to express your viewpoint.
- Show your palms and the insides of your elbows sometimes when you gesticulate. It enhances the sense of openness you are trying to project. In fact, when you combine it with uncrossed arms, it becomes a powerful quirk.
- There is a certain space called the 'confidence space.' It begins at the top of your chest and extends all the way down to your waist. Keep your gestures within

this space for maximum impact. Why?
When your gestures are placed within
this space, it shows that you are
confident, but in control of yourself. If
your gestures extend beyond this space,
then it might give the impression that
you are over-dramatic, uncontrollable, or
impulsive.

- Do not use gestures unless they serve a
  purpose. Otherwise, it might make you
  look comical.

- Your actions should not be robotic or
  stiff, as that shows a lack of confidence.
  Keep it fluid. In fact, a great trick is to
  know what gesture you have to make, but
  not focus on it. Your mind should be on
  the subject matter you are discussing.

- A neat trick you can use is to film
  yourself when you are talking with your
  friend or family member (with
  permission of course). When you record
  yourself and watch the video later, you
  will be able to find out what kind of
  gestures you perform when you are
  talking.

- Understand cultures when showing

gestures, especially if you are in another country. For example, crossing your fingers in the US and other English speaking countries is a sign of good luck, or hoping for good luck. However, in Vietnam, it refers to the female genitalia. So if you are in Vietnam and if someone asks you to wish them good luck, just don't cross your fingers.

Here are some that gestures you can employ to enhance your presentation skills.

- When counting or listing something, use your fingers to represent what number you are indicating. This movement not only anchors the attention of the viewer(s), but it allows you to mentally 'bookmark' what you should be saying next.
- To indicate a tiny quantity, bring your index finger as close to your thumb as possible without touching it. Some people also like to lower their neck and squint their eyes slightly to add a dramatic effect.

- When you want to imply a decision or if you want to emphasize something, you can bring the back of one hand to the palm of another. But make sure that you do not clap your hands loudly. Gently but firm taps are the way to go.

- In order to indicate 'everything' or 'wiping the slate clean,' you can move both your arms in a sweeping motion. The best way to perform this action is to only move your arms without having to move your upper body too much. By keeping your upper body slightly restricted, you are showing confidence. However, if you feel a certain tension in your body, making a dramatic gesture can help you alleviate it.

- When you want to differentiate between high and low, or small and large, then you can level your palm at different heights. For example, placing it at shoulder level indicates a high amount while keeping it at chest level indicates an average amount. A low quantity can be indicated by leveling your palm at your waist.

Remember that you can learn all the body language tricks in the world, but it won't do you any good if you don't have positivity. I know we already talked about positivity, but this time, I am referring specifically to your smile.

Practice your smile. It does not matter if you feel that you don't have an Oscar-winning smile: you can improve it.

Two of the most important aspects of a smile, according to science, are:

- The corners of the lips should be turned up.
- Eyes should crinkle, producing folds in the corners of your eyes called "crow's feet."

The second point is important because the formation of folds is involuntary. Not everyone who smiles is able to bring that crinkle at the corners of their eyes. However, that does not mean you cannot practice it. Stand in front of a mirror and hone your smile. Don't worry about how awkward the whole thing might seem. You would be surprised to know that many people, including famous celebrities, politicians, and people of importance, all practice their smile in front of a mirror. They do so because they might need to produce a smile whenever the occasion calls for it, even if they are not in the mental frame to smile.

This is especially true when you are greeting someone or shaking their hand. It is not easy to convey genuine warmth during greetings, especially when you are feeling terrible inside. Which is why practicing your smile helps you to quickly employ it when you need it.

You might master the smile, but you might fail at greetings, such as giving a handshake.

Your handshake should be firm, but not too strong. It should show confidence without making it seem as though you are holding a death grip.

People talk about your handshake, but only if it is bad. If you gripped someone's hands too tight, then they are bound to spread the word that you nearly crushed their body part. On the other hand, if your handshake is sloppy or weak, then people will talk about how you lack confidence.

If you find yourself in a position where you have given your best smile, but you don't know where to put your arms, you can mirror the other person. When you mirror the posture of the other person, you can connect with them better. This process builds trust and rapport with the person and allows you to communicate with others more openly.

However, having said that, you shouldn't try to mirror the other individual in an obvious manner, or they might wonder what you are up to. Let's say that the person speaking to you leans back while being seated. You should not be leaning forward at that moment. Lean back as well. As for your arms, even if the other person is keeping them crossed, you need to place them apart in a gesture of openness.

Before I end this chapter, I would like to impart one more suggestion for you.

Remember how I had mentioned earlier in one of my examples that I hadn't dressed as well as I should have for a business conference? I wouldn't recommend that. When you have the chance, take the time out to present yourself well to the world.

Let me put forth an example. Imagine if you had ordered something from Amazon, preferably an elec-tronic device. When it arrives at your doorstep, you are astonished to find that the component and all of its relevant parts have just been placed in the Amazon delivery package haphazardly, and not in its product package, like someone just tossed all the components into a bag and sent it over to you.

Now it does not matter whether the product is

functioning perfectly: you have still lost your confidence in it.

Everything, from your mannerisms to your character to your posture and other important traits, are components of you as a product. What binds it all together is your clothing. Call it your personality's 'packaging.' When the packaging is right, people greet you with more confidence. They have already decided that you are someone they should attend to or think about. You have impressed them.

When it comes to interviews, remember the below:

- Do not wear a suit to an interview, unless you are applying for a top-tiered position. If you wear a suit and the senior person interviewing you isn't in a suit, then it shows that you are in a more powerful position than the interviewer.
- Always opt to wear formal attire, minus the suit. If the interview calls for casuals, then under no circumstances should you sport a t-shirt and jeans. Instead, choose to wear semi-formal attire. You look presentable and you show the

interviewer that you are serious about working with them.

- Don't bring a huge bag like you are about to travel around the world, since it makes you look like someone who cannot plan things better. Neither should you be carrying your documents around with you in your hand; it shows carelessness. Take a small folder case with you. Women can carry a simple handbag.

- Stick to gray, blue, or black combinations as much as possible, and avoid bright colors. Muted greens and pinks can be used as well. Never make your outfit too colorful, such as throwing in a green and a blue piece of clothing together. Your top can be any of the colors we just mentioned, while your bottom attire should be grey, black, white, or cream.

4

CONNECT WITH YOUR AUDIENCE

*O*ne of the common mistakes that speakers do is to distance themselves from their audience. It creates a gap that makes it seem as though the speaker is in their own world or zone, and does not want to actively engage with the audience.

Before we start talking about how to effectively connect with your audience, let me talk to you about an important concept; energy. You see, your energy should be louder than your message.

And I am going to repeat that in case you thought I made a mistake. Your energy should be louder than your message.

History has shown us that even dictators were able to unite people under one banner, even though they had the wrong message to spread. But why resort to history. Let's take something much more personal: an interview. You may know the ideas you would like to present or the answers to the questions, but if you are not presenting them well, you are not going to change the minds of the interviewers. I have seen people with incredible qualifications be passed on for those with fewer qualifications. When I had questioned the interviewers about their choices, they would usually say that they felt that the candidate with fewer qualifications looked like he or she was capable of learning. They had a "good feeling" about him or her.

All this because the candidate just had a good personality and could command the audience's attention.

It's not about being smarter or being funnier. It is about having the energy that projects your personality to match your message.

But where does this energy come from? Do you need to down two cans of Red Bull in order to reach those levels? Or will half-a-can do?

Those questions present another problem – or rather, misconception – people have about energy. They think that when someone has energy, they have to be extremely active, jubilant, funny, or with a spring in their step. Nothing could be farther from the truth.

Energy is not about physical energy. Just take a look at public speeches by Jordan Peterson, or watch the TED Talk by Dolph Lundgren, the Hollywood actor. You will notice a sense of magnetic aura surrounding them. You feel as though you want to listen to them more. As you watch them, you will notice that their body language is poised and confident. Their gesticulations remain within the safe space. Their tone isn't loud and neither does it fluctuate too much: they just speak, and you are hooked.

What gives them this energy?

Before we delve into that, let's look at a few things you have to avoid doing.

Never judge people you haven't met. In fact, never judge people at all. Period. Do not target a person, always try to talk about their actions or words. It is very difficult to listen to someone who judges others, because deep down, you know that the person is judging you as well.

When you start judging people, the way you speak changes. There is an underlying sense of judgement that automatically slips into your message, even when you are not fully aware of it. However, just because you are not aware of it, does not mean that listeners won't be able to pick it out. The less you judge, the less chances you will have judgments slipping into your message.

Never produce too much negativity.

Nobody likes a negative person. We had already seen why it is important to have positivity. But have you wondered why negativity is bad?

When you add more negativity, your mind changes its perception about the world. You take on a cynical worldview, and that trickles down into your message, body language, and even actions. Some of the negativity can become so deeply embedded into your psyche that it becomes a part of your character. When that happens, it becomes difficult for you to project positivity.

When you are able to project positivity, remember to maintain a certain degree of humbleness.

You might have seen people enthusiastically talking about something as though it is true, while in your mind you are probably thinking, "I know this is wrong. Why am I even listening to this person?"

Dogmatism, when embedded into your personality, becomes a problem because you don't perform enough research and investigation to develop your points. You take something as fact, even though there is more evidence to prove that your point is wrong. Once you pick something to talk about, you vehemently defend it, even though the statement is false.

Sometimes, they use dogmatism to exaggerate something: exaggeration is used in certain mediums, such as in fiction and certain non-fiction. However, it is done so because in the absence of a person speaking to you, the words are the only method of expressing emotions. When writers want to express something, such as the intensity of a statement, they use exaggeration to get their point across.

For example, if I say "We have to do it!" while slapping my hands, then you know that whatever needs to be done is of utmost importance and contains urgency.

However, if I simply write "we have to do it", then I am not expressing that intensity. Is the speaker insisting that something should be done, or is he casually inferring something?

While exaggeration can serve a purpose in writing, it is a poor tool to use when speaking. More often than not, it comes across as 'fake' or even an outright lie. Use a combination of words and body language to get your point across.

PASSION AND VOICE

If you are passionate about something, allow yourself to show that passion. People don't like listening to someone who looks like he would rather be at the bar or at home watching tv.

When you are passionate about something, your face carries genuine emotions, and this is important, especially when you connect it with the earlier point about creating emotions in the audience. Those who love the topic they are talking about form emotions that the audience latch on to. By doing so, they don't have to put too much effort into evoking emotions in the audience: the job has already been done for them by the simple application of passion.'

You need to believe in your message in order for the audience to believe in it. The energy you apply into your speech or message is more or less proportionate to the attention that the audience provides you.

People can read your energy levels. If you don't feel like you want to be there, people will realize that. However, your levels of energy don't just depend on how active you are, but the way you employ your voice as well.

For example, you could look like you drank 8

cans of Red Bull, but if you speak in a monotonous voice, people might think that you don't have any energy.

Which is why I am going to reach out to your throat.

Okay, that did not sound right. Let me rephrase that. I am going to discuss some techniques that are going to reach out to your throat and activate an important mechanism there.

In your throat, you have a wonderful tool that is capable of applying so many techniques and skills in order to convey your message: your voice box. I'm going to take you through these tools and how important they are in creating an attractive message. Each of the tools will allow you to tune your message and connect with your audience better.

The first thing that we need to talk about is prosody.

Listen to a speech by Martin Luther King and you will feel like heading outside to spread the message of love and unity.

What makes his speeches so powerful that they can ignite fires in the minds of people?

It's the fact that he uses fluctuations in his voice, a technique referred to as prosody.

Let's take an example right here.

"Would you like a cup of tea?"

If you were reading that in your mind, chances are that you might have automatically raised the pitch of your voice by the time you reached the word tea, almost like English people do it. What you have done is using prosody, fluctuating your pitch based on the words you are saying or on the message you would like to convey.

For example, if you were to take the above – Would you like a cup of tea? – and use a monotonous voice to convey the question, there is no impact or emotion behind your message. You might as well be a Google voice program reading out your search results.

Prosody allows you to add depth, emphasis, and personality to your speech.

Here's another simple example:

Would YOU like to go out?

The emphasis is on the word 'you' and that could mean a lot of things. However, if you ask the same question in the manner below:

Would you LIKE to go out?

Now, you are trying to figure out the person's preferences. The change is subtle, but with the right emphasis, you can change the meaning of a sentence or question. Prosody allows you to manage these shifts in sentences so that you can control the messaging.

But prosody alone does nothing on its own. You need volume to control the intensity of prosody.

Not many people think about volume when they speak. However, you need to adjust your volume depending on the situation. For example, you can grab people's attention when you lower your voice. You are speaking as though you are revealing a confidential matter. It's like you want to bring everyone in on a secret that you don't want to share. You can then increase the volume of your voice when you want to emphasize something.

The increase and decrease of volume is something that you notice in politicians. When they are talking about a grave matter that affects them and the public, they lower their voice. But when they reach the part where they are talking about changes and reforms, the volume of their voice increases.

Control the volume in order to attract the audience's attention effectively.

Make sure that you are not speaking too fast if the situation does not require it.

When you are showing excitement, you can increase the pace at which you say something. On the other hand, you can slow down the pace of your speech, in order to emphasize something.

In today's world, some people like to increase their pace not because they want to create an effect, but because they want to squeeze as much information out as possible within a short period of time. Don't do that. You are not creating interest that way. Rather, you are bombarding the person with too much information that they begin to tune you out.

According to research, young adults can store anywhere from 3 to 5 chunks of information in their short-term memory. What do I mean by chunks?

Consider the below collection of letters and imagine someone throwing them at you at a fast pace:

FSBNPSFBIIRSKGB

Pretty confusing right? I can understand if you can't remember those letters.

Now imagine a second person walking up to you and repeating the above collection of letters, albeit at a slower pace, and arranging them in meaningful chunks.

FSB NPS FBI IRS KGB

All of a sudden, you understand the meaning of the seemingly random placement of letters. The letters above all represent a few popular organizations that a lot of people are familiar with. Now, you can remember the arrangement of letters.

By chunking information, you are able to deliver your message effectively. People remember what you have to say, and that attracts them towards you.

That does not mean that you should never speak fast. Just make sure that a faster pace serves a purpose, and does not throw too much information at someone.

Once you have mastered the use of voice to empower your message, you can also use certain techniques that will help you get your message across clearly. These techniques allow you to grab attention, evoke emotions, gain support, or achieve a plethora of goals through your message.

I was to give a speech during a friend's wedding day. There was no doubt about the fact that I would do it. Of course I would. My friend and I are like brothers. The speech itself is your typical Hollywood-style wedding speech: I compliment him, then I insult him, and then I insult him some more. Then I wish for the best in the couple's life.

When I was younger, I would never have dreamt of giving a speech like that, much less stand on a stage in front of a hundred or so people.

But that day, during my friend's wedding, I created a story.

THE ART OF STORYTELLING

There is more to storytelling than simply hooking the audience's attention. Through storytelling, you can evoke emotions, create anticipation, explain a complicated matter easily, approach a tough subject, or even create empathy with the audience.

Use many of the techniques mentioned in this book, from modulating your voice to commanding your posture, in order to tell your story. But also remember that your story should flow naturally. After all, it is a story, not the news.

When you are standing on the stage or when you have the spotlight in a social situation, you are either presenting yourself as an expert on the subject, or as someone who has something valuable to contribute. Simply laying down facts just to show that you are smart makes you seem arrogant. Instead, create a story using your life experiences and turn what could be a simple response into an engaging message, but don't make it seem like you are narrating the news. Let me give you an example.

You want to tell someone that in the core of the

sun, nuclear fusion takes place constantly. You can do it one of two ways.

Method 1:

"There is nuclear fusion occurring in the center of the sun where 700 million tonnes of hydrogen gets converted into 695 million tonnes of helium every second."

Method 2:

"I want you guys to think about what you are doing right now. Just think about how many seconds it takes to perform an action. How long does it take you? A second? A couple of seconds? Three? Let's think about your breathing. What if I told you right now that by the time you complete inhaling oxygen, 700 million tons of hydrogen just got converted to 695 million tons of helium in the core of the sun? Think about that. And that happens every single time you breathe. Inhale. 700 million tons of hydrogen to 695 million tons of helium. Exhale. 700 to 695. Over and over. All day long."

You see the difference? I guarantee that anyone who listens to Method 2 will be able to remember that fact about the core of the sun much better than those who listen to Method 1. Why? You didn't simply bombard them with information; they heard a story. You created anticipation and excitement. That's how powerful storytelling can be.

But what aspect of Method 2 made it so engaging and compelling? Why was it better than Method 1?

To put it simply, it was the emotions it evoked.

When you are using emotions, you are reaching out for the audience's empathy. You take them on an emotional journey, from suspense to excitement, from joy to revelation, or from something absurd to something even more ridiculous. The point is, storytelling moves people.

But how do you build a good story?

You first have to ask yourself what conclusion you are hoping to create. Joy? Sadness? What is it that you are hoping to achieve by the end of the speech?

Then start moving backwards to the beginning. How do you start the story in order to get the desired result? If you are aiming to create joy, for example, then do you start with a joke? Or would you rather tell a sad tale that slowly turns into a happy ending?

Once you have formed the approach, think about how you can weave the story to fit the emotional journey you have created. You can even create a story arc to get your emotional content right.

If you can create a story around a story arc, you can attract the attention of your audience better.

- A good story starts with an introduction. You can create a bang or you can ease the audience into something. Start with a fact. Tell a personal story. Talk about statistics.

- You then move on to the development. Here, you explain the point of your speech. Add more details to help the audience understand what you want to say. But remember, it's Method 2 and not Method 1 you should be using.

- Next, reach the climax of your story. This is the point just before the conclusion. You take this opportunity to bring all the facts together and to include any additional information that you think the audience should know.

- Finally, you reach the resolution, the meaning of your message, the results of your studies, or the end of your story. Whatever you are hoping to accomplish, you do so at this point.

To be fair, you might not use all of the above story arc points. For example, you might not require the climax at all. You could skip the step-in order to reach the conclusion. But in essence, if you follow the story arc, you will have a better grasp on how to arrange information.

This is true whether you are communicating a simple piece of information or a complicated topic.

Although, when it comes to a complicated topic, then people often wonder how they can create interest in the audience. What can you do to keep them engaged for a long period of time, when your content is packed with information?

I am an astronomy fan. There is something exciting about learning more about supernovas, nebulas, and neutrinos. When I talk about the subject, I am truly passionate about it and people respond to that. They are curious to know more about the subject. They want me to add more details. Often, I find myself staring at faces displaying rapt attention.

However, there is something else I do to make sure that the listeners are engaged. You see, I don't just show passion for the subject matter, I try to make it easy to understand.

I know that not a lot of people are aware of the

information that I am going to present to them. It's rather novel, and it takes time to understand the various concepts. When people are fed too much information that makes understanding difficult or if the speaker is not capable of explaining things properly, they lose interest. But the reality is that astronomy is a fairly complicated subject. It's not easy to simply explain something.

That is when I use information that the audience is familiar with.

For example, when I want to talk about supernova – the explosion of a star – I start with a simple question:

You guys know that stars explode right? I mean, they have shown that in quite a few Hollywood movies.

See what I did there? I used a simple fact that the audience is more familiar with to create a connection. Now, I can slowly ease into the more difficult aspects of the topic. Even when I am fully into the topic, I periodically sprinkle commonly-known information in my speech. I don't want to lose the audience and I want them to know that I am talking about something they know about, or something they will find easy to know about.

I also pay attention to the audience. I want to

truly know how they respond to what I say. Are they really interested, or are they dozing off?

You see, speakers are truly self-conscious. But it is for a good reason. They have to juggle the topic while making sure that the audience is interested.

There is just one more trick you can use to ensure the audience is still with you. Firstly, become aware of the responses of the audiences. Are they looking bored? Are they agreeing with you? Do some of them disagree?

I was once talking about visiting Bali to some of my friends. The subject began to circle around street food, since I mentioned having a delicious bowl of Nasi Goren – or Indonesian fried rice – from a street vendor. I noticed that one of my friends crinkled his face in disgust, obviously worried about the hygiene of the street vendor.

Rather than ignore it, I approached it with empathy and understanding.

I told him, "I understand how you feel and I am cautious of the unhygienic conditions of certain street vendors. However, this vendor was in a rather upscale part of the city. In fact, the entire theme of his food outlet was to create authenticity. So his choice of looking like a street vendor was deliberate."

Instantly, my friend was engaged. In fact, he

went on to ask me where he could find this street vendor and taste authentic Indonesian food, since he wanted to travel to Bali as well.

Here is an important thing that you should know about responding to audiences; make sure that you are understanding and empathetic. Don't attack anyone.

There are many different people around the world. Each one has their own tastes, preferences, and beliefs. Just because someone does not share the same viewpoint as you, it does not mean they are horrible people. Understand that they are just like you, with a difference in opinion. When you think that way, you automatically remove negativity from your body and look at the world using a little more optimism. And optimism allows you to respond to your audience much better than negativity.

When you notice a particular reaction, think about how you can address it without appearing antagonistic.

5

BEGIN WITH THE END IN MIND

I referred to beginning with the end under the Storytelling section. But what does that mean?

What many people fail to do is that they don't think about the conclusion. They have no idea where their message or speech should lead. What is the point that they are trying to prove? What message would they like to impart on the audience? Is there a fact that they would like to reveal to the audience?

Without a goal in mind, your message can meander into unknown and, quite frankly, unwanted territories. You may not know how to anchor your thoughts. The information is going to keep flowing and you are unsure how to conclude. When the audience realizes that you are not going to conclude anytime soon, they will create the conclusion for you, by either ignoring you or moving on.

I know that most of you are going to point out that I have provided an example of lawyers and how they speak extemporaneously. I agree with that approach, but lawyers go in blind. They don't make things up on the spot. Well, they do sometimes, but only when they are well aware of what they have to say and the conclusion they have to reach.

In other words, while it is true that they merely create an overall outline of their speech, they practice that outline as much as possible.

The reason lawyers' practice is because they want to have a mental guideline in order to talk about different topics. They know the result they want to reach and the steps they have to take to reach there. With the information that they have, even if they have to skip a few steps, they can do so without hesitation. After all, they have practiced all the steps in their presentation. They don't mind backtracking or fast-forwarding towards certain points.

Why is it important to practice? For one, you avoid awkward phrases.

Maybe you don't do it intentionally, but there are certain automatic phrases that you employ which might not do well in certain situations. Identifying them helps you watch out for them.

For example, I used to have the habit of saying "trust me" quite often.

- Trust me, I have been there and I know it.
- Trust me when I tell you, that is not the right way to do it.

The problem with the "trust me" statement is that you have created a boundary at the point you used the phrase. You are saying that before that boundary, anything you said shouldn't be trusted. It is only after you said "trust me" that people should start putting their faith in your words.

Ask yourself this; was everything you said before the "trust me" point untrustworthy? Then why would you especially use that phrase in the middle of the message or speech. On the other hand, if you use it in the beginning of the speech or message, it shows that you are going to provide conclusions, statements, and ideas based on personal feelings, not facts or figures. And that might not be a prudent course of action in certain scenarios.

When I understood my habit, I began to watch

out for it. When I was asked to present a business proposal, I remember feeling the temptation to say "trust me." But because I was aware of it, I stopped myself from saying it. Instead, I chose to show proof and explain why my potential partner should trust me. And guess what? He was convinced even before I reached the conclusion.

Practicing your outline helps you identify such awkward phrasing and eliminate it entirely. Your speech becomes tight and you are able to project more confidence at the same time.

Also remember to never say more than is absolutely necessary. Nobody likes it when people go on and on about a particular subject. If you are unaware of the structure of your message, then you don't know when to end a particular section or even what direction to take the message. Try this exercise:

1. Create a structure using the story arc method. Under each part of the arc, write down the points that you would like to talk about.

2. Stand in front of a mirror and start your timer. Practice talking about each section in your story arc outline. You don't have to memorize the points. Write them on a

piece of paper and refer to them whenever you like. As you talk about each point, you will realize that some points require more information than others. Don't do anything about them for now. Continue explaining your points. Do not worry about the timer.

3. Once you have completed the presentation or speech, check the time. If you were comfortably within a certain time limit, you have nothing to worry about. However, if you were close to or crossed the time limit, then you might have to edit your information. Ask yourself:

4. Can you keep the information in the longer sections concise? Perhaps you can merge two points together.

5. Are there any points you can remove entirely?

6. Do you think you could provide bullet point styled information instead of a long explanation?

7. Edit and rearrange your presentation. Once again, use the timer to check how long it takes to deliver the message.

8. Repeat the above process as many times as you like in order to reach a satisfying presentation duration.

And do check your energy levels.

It is one thing to say that you are going to add as much energy as possible into your presentation and quite another to actually pull it off.

One of the best ways to gauge your energy levels is to actually practice the outline. You might figure out where your energy levels dip. When you reach such a point, ask yourself these questions:

- Do you really have to add that point into your presentation?
- Can you replace the point with something else that can add more value?
- Is there any way you can make it more interesting, perhaps by turning it into a story or adding a joke?
- How about turning the point into a question in order to pique the audience's attention?

Once you have handled the above points, I

would also like you to invite someone to help you practice.

Practicing your speech by yourself is good. But practicing it in front of someone who can provide you with honest feedback is much better. There are so many reasons to bring someone into your practice sessions:

- Is your humor on point or do you have to refine it? Will people find it offensive?
- Were you able to keep the attention of the participant throughout your presentation?
- As you are giving your presentation, are you able to notice any feedback, in the form of nodding heads, smiles, or other physical actions?

Once you have finished your speech, you can sit with the participant and then ask him or her these questions:

- How did you find the presentation overall?
- What was your favorite part of the presentation and why?

- What did you find annoying or displeasing? What did you find boring?
- Is there anything you would change about my presentation?
- Were you able to understand the points I brought up in the presentation?

Once you collect all the above feedback, fine tune your presentation. Conduct additional research so that you have all the information that you need.

In fact, you should present yourself as an expert on your topic. In order for you to do that, you need to research your topic well.

One of the best ways to do this is during the outline phase. After you have written down the points of your presentation, ensure that you know how to talk about them fluently and informatively.

If you think that there are certain points that you are not confident talking about, don't include them in your presentation. It is far better to not talk about something than to pretend to know about it and fumble your way through the presentation.

I remember once talking about posture to an audience. When I was going through the exercises, I made it a point to tell them how you can make your back straight. I even briefly highlighted a fact about the spine, but I honestly mentioned that I wouldn't get into the technical aspects. I wasn't going to pretend that I knew the details of what I was going to say, even though I knew that I was right, and I could even provide a resource to back up my claims.

Don't be afraid to avoid getting too much into the details of certain aspects. I am not saying that you should honestly admit you know nothing about a subject. That is quite harmful for your presentation and the general idea is, if you don't know about the topic, why present it at all in the first place?

Present the topic. Don't feel compelled to dive into too many details. Besides, details can sometimes bore the audience.

But that does not mean that you have to speak fast in order to get to the good parts of the presentation.

Remember what we talked about pace? Here is something you should try to remember. It is preferable that you slow down, especially when you are giving a presentation. Now I am not saying that speeding up is a bad thing. But if you notice, I mentioned increasing your pace if it serves a purpose.

When you talk slowly, you are showing that you are in no rush to cover the topic. And you know the kind of people who are not in a rush? Those who are confident.

Confident people know that they are masters of their topics. They don't want to speed through the topic and confuse everyone in the audience. They take things slowly, like a master storyteller.

Now I know a lot of you are wondering about the timing aspect of the presentation. After all, didn't we discuss how to keep the message or information within a certain duration?

Once again, this is where the act of practicing your speech or presentation comes into play. When you are practicing, speak in a measured and controlled pace. Don't be so slow that the audience are going to wish they were in a coma instead. And neither should you be so fast that people are going to wonder if they should record what you are saying and play it later in slow motion.

Practice your speech using a controlled pace and then start editing or trimming your presentation.

You need to be able to combine both content and pace within the time period. In the end, it is not just about the message, but also about how you deliver that message.

VISUALIZE SUCCESS

I know this might sound like a random tip thrown in here, but it serves a very important purpose. Too often, people walk on to the stage expecting criticism and complaints. They have formed a negative idea about the audience and that negativity feeds itself. Eventually, these people try too hard, or forget what they should be saying, or even fumble through facts. They make mistakes even though they have practiced their presentation really well.

Remember how I had talked about going to Bali and trying Nasi Goreng? Well, I was in Germany once and was sampling their sauerbraten, a stew made of roast beef. Imagine if I told you that the dish was bland: you would now have a negative idea about it. It does not matter whether you believe me or not; you would build your expectations from a negative point, and that would not allow you to wholly enjoy the food. If I had told you that you should try sauerbraten because it is delicious (spoiler alert: it is actually delicious), you would dig into the dish with a lot more eagerness.

It's the same with a presentation or a speech. When you have a negative expectation, the level of motivation you provide yourself won't be too strong.

It might just be a half-hearted attempt at making yourself feel better.

However, picture yourself succeeding at giving the presentation or speech. Think about walking on to the stage and grabbing everyone's attention or making them laugh. Visualize success.

When you step on a stage, it does not matter if you feel nervous, if you make a mistake, or if you fumble a bit: you are going to correct these hiccups with poise and confidence. You are going to radiate positivity.

Naomi Campbell is one of the most popular supermodels in the world. But what made her so famous is not just her beauty, but her personality. She was once walking down the runway when she accidentally tripped and fell. Typically, that would have been an extremely embarrassing situation for any model to be in. They would have embarrassingly picked themselves off and completed their walk in a cloud of awkwardness. But not Naomi. She picked herself up, laughed at her own mistake, and continued down the runway.

So much positivity and confidence.

And that is why you need to focus on the idea that you are going to be successful.

There are also a few things that you can do to get

a good head start. Each presentation is unique, so pick the option that fits the message and theme of your presentation, speech, or message.

What are some of the tricks that you can use in order to start your presentation or speech well (or even a conversation)?

- Start with a statement that immediately grabs the attention of the audience. This can be done through a surprising fact, or a daring statement.
- Use a joke to lighten the mood. However, do note that jokes are not always appropriate for a serious topic. Make sure you understand your topic well before trying to be funny.
- You can even start with the conclusion and slowly guide your audience towards that conclusion.
- Narrate a personal story, especially if you have a personal connection to the topic you are speaking about. I should warn you that simply adding a personal story when that story serves no purpose is going to confuse the audience.
- You can start the presentation or speech

using a quote from someone well-known. It helps the audience understand the tone of the presentation.

- If there is a problem that you are going to solve, then begin by addressing the problem.
- Ask rhetorical questions. It gives the audience something to think about before you launch into your monologue.

6

OVERCOME SHYNESS

*O*f course, one cannot put into practice many of the suggestions mentioned in this book if they are feeling shy or overwhelmed about facing a large crowd. Shyness is something that requires a bit of attention. You can't erase it within a short period of time. However, you can gradually work on it until you are comfortable enough to overcome it.

When you feel shy, then you are feeling uncertain about yourself. You are not sure if your actions, words, or emotions are right for the moment. More importantly, you are worried that you are going to embarrass yourself, cause further harm, or say something inappropriate. All of these negative reactions overwhelm you so much that you lose sight of the fact that all you have to do is rationally evaluate the situation and form a response. All that uncertainty causes you to become shy. But that is not the only reason for shyness.

People feel shy for a myriad of reasons.

For example, many are of the opinion that shyness is a temperamental issue and it is present because of psychological reasons. However, what if I were to tell you that there is evidence to prove that genes play an important role in how shy you can be? That is not to say that genetics is the cause in each and every situation. The environment plays an important role in molding our personalities as well. Additionally, family dynamics and past relationships also play a huge part in developing someone's personality.

The good news is that eliminating shyness might just be possible.

There are two methods to eliminate shyness:

- You practice working on it at a moment when you are not feeling shy.
- You deal with it as it happens.

Let's go through each method.

We will start with the method that requires a bit of practice.

The more you practice, the more you will be able to understand your shyness. And the more understanding you have about your behavior, the better you are able to deal with it. Remember that shyness is an internal factor, and you need to connect with those factors.

When you connect with your inner self, you have a better sense of who you are and how to express yourself. You begin to feel more comfortable in your own presence and express passion when talking about the subjects that matter to you.

But how can you speak from the heart?

Pick a topic that you are passionate about. You can even pick someone you would like to talk to.

Once you are ready, follow the below ideas to prepare yourself.

- Make sure that you are grounded in well thought-out intentions. For example, you want to talk about your subject matter because you want to share it with someone. Or maybe because you just love to explore it. It could also be because you want to help someone or make a difference.

- After you have created good intentions for your message, get an idea of what you want to say. Think about your personal experience on the subject, such as your thoughts, feelings, memories, ideas, desires, reactions, and other factors.

- Use the steps mentioned in Chapter 5 to create an outline and practice your presentation. Don't try to be anything other than your natural self. If possible, record yourself speaking since it allows you to fine tune your presentation skills.

- Most importantly, trust in your level of sincerity. You are going to passionately speak about a particular subject, not commit a crime. Don't doubt yourself.

- You are going to edit the way you speak later, in order to fine-tune your presentation skills, so go ahead and speak as much as you want on the topic.

But don't just speak to someone you are comfortable speaking to.

This might be a little difficult, but try to speak

out more in social situations. Do not worry whether things are going to be awkward or not. The reason is that you won't know what you are doing wrong if you do not allow yourself to communicate.

Of course, in many cases, the awkward social interactions can drive a torpedo through any confidence that people might have. In such cases, what can you do?

- Start small. If you feel uncomfortable talking for lengthy periods of time, then make small contributions. The more emboldened you become, the more resistance you build against criticism.
- Speaking of criticism, start evaluating yourself. If you notice that there is a part of your approach that you would like to improve, do not hesitate to do so. When you recognize areas you want to improve, you identify the parts that you would like to change. Even if someone else points it out to you, it won't affect you as much as it would have.

I would like to touch on the above point a little more. Usually, novel and unfamiliar situations can bring about shyness in a person. However, if you seek out the areas of your communication and personality you would like to improve, it will not be unfamiliar territory anymore. If someone were to talk about it, then it wouldn't surprise you. You are already familiar with that part and hence, you can reduce the levels of shyness you feel. On the other hand, if you do not acknowledge the parts of yourself that you would like to improve and someone talks about it, it might take you by surprise. And that surprise in turn can create extreme shyness.

- Accept that fact that you are not going to be as dynamic as an outgoing or sociable person instantly. Your improvements are going to show themselves gradually. Accept the progress you make and use it to the fullest.
- Try to talk about subject matters that you are not familiar with. Perform your own research on those subjects and present your own unique take on it.

Finally, I want you to repeat this: socially awkward situations aren't life-threatening. Don't think of them as an end to something. Know that the way the world is progressing, people are more open and accepting towards unique personality traits. The rate at which people are quickly judging others is decreasing.

Remember this: it is okay for some people to not like you. It is completely normal, and you may not like everyone that you come across either. I honestly recommend that you avoid trying to impress everyone you meet. That may become too stressful because you would be trying to please too many people at once.

Think about it this way; even famous people like Ryan Reynolds and Emily Blunt have haters. Heck, you just have to go on YouTube and check out 'celebrity mean tweets' to know just how much insulting people can be to celebrities.

Make peace with the fact that people are going to dislike you, no matter what, but remember that they don't decide the kind of person you are. Only you have the power to do that to yourself.

But that also presents another problem. People who are shy do have the power to decide what kind of people they are, but they make false assumptions about themselves.

What makes things worse for people who are shy is that they tend to overanalyze their situation. They try to dig deep into their actions and find out why they did what they did.

After that comes the part that destroys their confidence: they try to fantasize about what they could have done right.

Thinking about "what ifs" is a surefire way to create more doubt and fear into your mind. Stop allowing yourself to project your solutions into a hypothetical situation in your mind. Go out and exercise those solutions that you thought of.

Additionally, I would also like you to resist those thoughts as much as possible. Instead, I would like you to evaluate yourself from a practical standpoint. Think about what you would like to improve and make notes about it. Then apply your solutions in practice.

If you find it difficult putting your learnings into practice, start small.

What if you can't even bring yourself to shake hands with people? Then the issue does not merely lie with the fact that you are shy: it is about building up the courage to take actions. You need to develop your will so that it can push down your fear.

When people talk about courage, they think it means the absence of fear. That is not true. When there is no fear, it means you are fearless, which does not automatically equate to courage.

Courage is measured in the presence of fear, when you are afraid but are still able to temper it and continue your course of action. Courage is about helping yourself, but also making sure you are helping others in the process. This might not happen all the time, but a sense of empathy goes hand-in-hand with having courage for the right reasons.

So how do you build courage? Start with your presentation.

If you don't care how you present yourself, you are teaching your mind to pay little attention to yourself. That can have disastrous results because your mind will learn to ignore you.

Make a list of things that are vital to your hygiene. These could include something as simple as brushing your teeth twice a day, and taking at least one shower every day. Set a time for these activities. Every day, make sure that you complete the tasks at the time that you have chosen. Once you have gotten used to a certain schedule, start taking extra care of yourself. Work out at home or head to the gym. Keep yourself physically fit. The goal here is not to build layers upon layers of muscle, but to keep your body healthy. There is truth in the saying about how when you keep a healthy body, you keep a healthy mind.

Once you have taken care of your presentation, it's time for you to actually start talking. Initially, I would like you to practice honesty.

I am not referring to the fact that you have to walk up to someone and say, "My goodness, how ugly you look today."

I think such honesty would definitely get you in trouble. What I am referring to is honesty tempered with kindness, compassion, love, and generosity. When you have good intentions, you begin to feel more sure about yourself. After all, if someone dislikes you for your good actions, words, or intentions, then how can it be your fault that something is wrong? It's the other person's fault for thinking negatively about you. Soon, you will stop projecting negativity to yourself. Your kindness and love will extend to include you as well.

Additionally, the more of the positive traits that I just mentioned you practice, the more you are able to add that into the way you speak and conduct presentations as well. Once you notice positivity in your speeches and presentations, you begin to gain even more confidence in yourself and your abilities.

The more confidence you get, the more you will be able to handle your fears as well.

When you have a certain fear, take time to think about it and address it. The first question you have to ask is whether the fear is rational or not.

Fear is a defense mechanism that the body adopts in order to keep us safe. Sometimes, that safety is not required and might prove to be an inconvenience. Which is why you need to ask yourself these questions:

- Is it truly necessary to feel fear at a particular moment? Can I not handle myself without having to rely on my body's automated mechanisms?
- Do I feel the presence of threat in the situation? Am I going to receive bodily harm or deep psychological trauma?
- What am I truly afraid of?

Once you have addressed your fear, don't just lock it away. Rather, handle it next time. Create a solution for the fear. For example, if your fear says that you are a nervous wreck every time you talk to someone, rather than believe your thoughts, try to think about how you can deal with it. The next time you are in a social situation, go ahead and talk to someone. Don't pretend to be funny or bold. Just be yourself (remember: kindness, compassion, love, and generosity). Allow yourself to act like a human being with good intentions. Afterwards, ask yourself these questions:

- Did you talk with respect and politeness?
- Was the other individual behaving in a manner that might be rude, crass, or simply insensitive?
- Did you try your best to engage with people?

As you begin to ask these questions, try not to place yourself in the default victim's position. You see, people who are shy turn the blame on themselves through force of habit. They don't like blaming themselves, yet they haven't trained themselves to look at things from another perspective.

And that is what we are going to change today. However you choose to answer, use logical reasonings. Let's take an example.

Did you try your best to engage with people?

Your answer should be along these lines:

I tried to. However, I believe I did not engage as

much as I could have. My shyness still continued to hold me back. I did feel confident about the way I smiled genuinely at people. I did feel embarrassed at one point because I did not know much about the topic. Though I think I can rectify that by actually showing curiosity for learning more. So instead of feeling awkward, I could ask the person to explain his stance.

See what you did there? There was no blame thrown around and neither did you feel bad about something. All you did was give a proper reason as to why something could have happened, and a follow-up solution.

Always create a solution in the end. Do not leave things hanging, since that will make you feel as though some problems don't have any solutions.

If you think that you cannot find a solution on your own, then ask for help. Remember that you don't have to tackle all your problems on your own. Sometimes, it is okay to ask for help. That fact alone should help you feel better: just because some obstacles seem insurmountable, you don't have to feel defeated. There are ways you can deal with them. Using the idea that you can always seek help, face your challenges head-on. The more you start facing challenges, the more courage you develop.

In fact, you can even learn how to be more coura-geous by asking others for help.

If your friend, parent, or a person you know displays a sense of courage when dealing with prob-lems, ask them how they do it.

Here are three questions that you can ask them:

- How do you tackle a difficult problem?
- What do you do when things become overwhelming or the task becomes too difficult?
- How do you deal with fear?

Then you can apply their logic into your life.

STAND UP FOR YOURSELF

In the first chapter, I had mentioned a personal expe-rience of mine where someone insulted me by using a derogatory word. However, name-calling is just one of the ways people can attack you. Some people may try to undermine your position, while others may try to lessen the value of your accomplishments. If you feel attacked, stand up for yourself. Don't let people get a free pass for their words or actions.

Only you can decide what is acceptable for

people to say or do to you. That is why, you need to set boundaries.

When you set boundaries, you begin to maintain a certain threshold and tolerance for other people's words and behavior. If someone crosses that boundary, you have to be willing to walk away. Don't give them the time or attention. Let them know that they are not supposed to say or do what they just did.

Let's say for example that a co-worker is often making you the butt of his or her jokes. The jokes themselves do not cut too deep, but they are repeated so often, that you are worried that you are going to be considered as something you are not. If that happens, stand up and walk away.

That's it. Don't worry about the effect you have on them. After all, they weren't worried about the effect their words had on you.

When talking to people, remember to maintain a straight posture: chest in front of your shoulders and not the other way around, hands free to express themselves.

When you have a strong body language, people are going to assume that you are a strong and confident person. When you use body language, you are physically telling people to not take advantage of you. It's like a giant signpost that says: just because I tolerate, does not mean you take advantage.

Apart from posture, there are two key points to remember:

- Maintain eye contact. A good way to do this is by either picking one of the eyes of the person and then looking at it. If you start looking from one eye to the next, then you look shifty. And that in turn places you in your head with worries about whether you are making the right eye contact, whether you're coming off as creepy, if there is something else you should be doing, and so on. When you get in your head, it is a difficult place to get out of.
- Speak from your chest. Feel the vibrations spread across your upper torso. It is okay if you haven't spoken from the chest before. You can always practice. Use breathing exercises and upper body exercises, and then speak slowly and confidently.

When it comes to body training, people automatically imagine lifting weights and holding dumbbells. The truth is, if you cannot, for whatever reason, access equipment, you can use your home or another private space to workout or perform some exercises.

Let me throw in a simple routine you can follow every day:

- 20 squats
- 15 second plank
- 10 push-ups
- 30 jumping jacks
- 10 lunges for each leg

You don't have to follow the above routine. Create your own routine based on your requirements, but make sure that you follow it every day diligently.

Try doing things that take you out of your comfort zone. It could be anything from participating in a game of basketball with complete strangers to joining an activity club. When you start pushing yourself to face challenges you have never faced before, then you slowly start desensitizing yourself towards shyness.

The more you become desensitized, the more you build up your courage. In the future, if you were to face conflicts or if you had to say something to someone, then you won't hesitate as much, or you won't dilute your message.

Speaking of dilution: know when to filter your messages. When you are speaking to someone, you have to always be cautious of what you say. Kindness, compassion, generosity, and empathy – keep these four traits in mind.

On the other hand, when you want to warn someone off from doing something, then you shouldn't dilute your message too much. It is okay to say:

I don't appreciate you saying that.

Instead of:

You see, I don't mind that people make fun of me. In fact, I enjoy it and I am a good sport most of the time. But sometimes I feel slightly offended because of certain words or actions. They remind me of something that happened in the past.

You might find yourself adopting the second form of response. But you don't owe anybody any explanation. People don't give you an explanation for the words they use or the actions they take. Why should you explain anything?

Someone caused offense. And it is okay to simply

tell them that they did. You don't have to include additional information.

But what do you do when you face shyness suddenly? You are talking to a group of people, when someone says or does something, and you find yourself feeling shy. How can you stop the feeling from over-powering you? What tips can you implement when you haven't prepared yourself for dealing with shyness?

When you recognize the moment of shyness, and when you have no ideas what to say, where to place your hands, or even what to do next, then simply stop trying to do something.

That's really it. Just pause for a moment to catch your breath or simply take in your surroundings. Alternatively, if you were interrupted by a person, focus your attention on the individual.

For example, let's say that you are at a bar or a club and you get separated from your friends. Or perhaps they leave to take care of something. During those moments, you might feel compelled to do something. Should you introduce yourself to some-one? Do you have to move your body to the music, so that you don't look left out?

The answer is, just don't do anything for 20 to 30 seconds. You are removing any obligation to act or say something. When you become overwhelmed with shyness, then your psychological defenses are screaming at you to say or do something. When you give in, you might make things worse for yourself, or create additional stress.

Just relax. Look around you. Observe the environment or listen to someone else talk. Remember, you don't have to feel obligated to say or do something. Silence is a wonderful response as well.

And don't forget to stand up for yourself. I am once again going to remind you of the example from earlier in the book about how someone had called me a p***y. But I know that things might be slightly different if you are suddenly overcome with shyness. So how do you react in the spur of the moment?

Firstly, acknowledge that you have been offended or that you are not in a comfortable situation at that moment. It allows you to get past the conflict of whether you are feeling good at that moment or not. In fact, it is that inner conflict of deciding what you should be feeling that paralyzes you and makes you feel even more shy.

At the same time, you might not want to come out as aggressive or in the mood to start a conflict. What do you do then?

I would like you to think about the situation and

why it made you feel upset, sad, or brought about any other negative emotion.

For example, if you were in a group and discussing ideas for a road trip and someone says, "That is such a s**tty idea. Come up with something more interesting."

At this point, you can feel the shyness slowly building up inside you. Don't allow it to overwhelm you. Think about the person's response. What did he or she say? Was it really rude? Do you know this person so well that they can talk to you like that?

If no, then simply reply back by saying:

I can understand that if it is not a good idea, but I would appreciate it if you weren't so crass about it.

On the other hand, if someone is putting you down too much, then simply say:

I feel like you are being too negative about this.

When you begin to respond to people crossing boundaries slightly, you begin to grow more confident in yourself. You understand that you are a human being with likes, dislikes, preferences, and ideas. It is okay for you to have them. It is not okay for someone to trample on them through words or actions without your permission.

You need to understand that people shouldn't be taking advantage of you.

Often we are stuck in our head, and we are unable to get out of that confined space where ideas are constantly bombarding us.

You should stop listening to the voices in your head, because they are always telling you what you should do, and what you shouldn't, and that cluster of information can be quite overwhelming, and confusing. When things get overwhelming, then you won't know whether you are being taken advantage of, because you are too busy dealing with the chaos in your head.

But how can one step out of their own head?

Bring your attention to your body. Think about your hands or your facial expressions. You are transferring your attention from the things inside you, to the things outside you.

For example, if you are in a meeting, you can focus on your hands first. Make sure that they are in an open position. Softly take a few deep breaths. Feel the oxygen enter your lungs, your diaphragm, and all the way to your pelvis. Then focus on your facial expressions and see if you are showing interest, or if the situation demands, add a smile to your face.

You can also look at the speaker, turning your body to face him or her as a sign of attention. This not only allows you to control your actions, but it also has a positive effect on the speaker, who might be thankful or appreciative of the fact that you are paying attention.

When you start to bring various actions under control, you are gaining more power over your body. The more power you get, the farther you push yourself away from your thoughts. And that is what we want to achieve. We are forcing out negative feedback and embracing the positive ones.

This allows you to avoid feeling overwhelmingly shy in the moment.

Sometimes however, you might be successful in purging the shyness out of your body, but it does not mean the feeling is gone forever. It could return at a later time.

One of the things that you can do to seal in your confidence and lock away shyness is to take action. Find someone who is receptive of what you would like to say and speak to them. If you are in a social situation, look for someone you would love to talk to and someone who is not too busy to listen to you, then start a conversation with that person. Alternatively, you can become inquisitive. For example, if you are in the middle of the conversation, then you can pose a question or clarify a doubt.

What you are looking for is a source of reception

for your ideas, thoughts, or words. When you find that reception, you simply engage with that person.

I would take this method one step further. When you have free time, especially before the event, try to prepare some conversation starters. The reason is that when the time comes for you to exercise *Reception*, then you won't have to go back in your head. After all, that's where all the confusing and chaotic ideas are present, and they only make things worse for you. If you have a few practiced questions or conversation starters, use them.

But what if you don't have any? What if you are not prepared beforehand? Then I would like you to focus on the words of the speaker. Understand the meaning of what they are saying. Make proper eye contact. Keep your body loose. Then think of a question that you can ask or a supporting comment you can make about their comments.

Here's an example.

I was at a party once when I became part of this small group of people who were listening to one person talk about his experiences with a Lamborghini.

At that time, I was still a fairly shy person, but I had trained myself to use various techniques to avoid shyness.

So when I started feeling shy, I started listening to the person intently. At one point, he said something that sounded surprising. Rather than keep quiet, I exclaimed by saying, "Oh wow."

It was a simple statement. Yet the effect was instantaneous. The person turned to me and said, "It's crazy right?"

"Absolutely. I can't believe you did that," I said.

The person laughed. I received reception for my words. The fact that they had a positive effect on someone made me feel good about myself. The best part was that I was more confident to talk to people or, at the very least, respond to people for the rest of the evening. Even when I didn't respond or talk to anyone, I didn't feel bad about it or feel shyness overcome me. I was feeling positive because of one encounter.

Another good way to implement *Reception* is by acknowledging someone. If you notice people talking about something difficult, genuinely give them your attention. Not only will you help them, but you are using the 'stop' reaction to stop doing anything. Your whole attention is now honed in on the other person. A simple "I understand" or "I see" can help you connect with someone.

Everyone likes a positive response. Yet most

people are not willing to do anything in order to get positivity.

When you express gratitude, you acknowledge that there are good things in your life. From a psychological perspective, gratitude helps people receive more happiness. It automatically releases positive emotions in people, and these emotions can be a potent force in dispelling shyness.

At the end of the day, badly-timed shyness is a negative feeling. It cripples your chances to make connections, prevents you from speaking out, and does not allow you to truly experience the moment.

The solution? More positivity.

Never think of gratitude as a submissive reaction. When you are grateful, you don't show a lack of confidence. In fact, the word 'gratitude' is derived from the word gratia, a Latin word that translates to grace.

When you show gratitude, you are being grace-ful. You are showing people that you are not hesitant about being thankful about someone or something, showing your appreciation, or returning kindness. People are drawn towards such confidence.

Plus, let's not forget the fact that gratitude helps you forge stronger relationships. You make better friends, you can easily connect with people and, of course, you can become part of conversations smoothly (important if you suddenly feel shyness trying to overpower your thoughts).

BONUS TIPS

Here are some other things that you can do to avoid shyness.

- Avoid labeling yourself as shy. The more you do it, the more the word 'shy' becomes a fixture in your mind. And that does not help you distance yourself away from it. Even if you display certain behavioral patterns that resemble shyness, don't say you are shy. Instead, think of yourself as building courage. That has a more positive effect on you.

- Sometimes, we are our worst enemy. Our mind tells us that we are not doing something right, even though it could be something as simple as saying "thank you", or showing kindness. Never self-sabotage your attempts at removing shyness. If you have good intentions and you genuinely mean well for someone, do what you set out to do, despite your mind's interference.

- Forge strong relationships. It is not always about the quantity of people in your life, but their quality also matters. Spend time with people who are able to give you positive responses.

- Watch and learn. It is okay to observe someone in order to try and learn the way they approach conversations or situations. You can then apply any learnings in your own life. Of course, you may have to modify what you learnt in order to fit the scenarios you face, but there is no harm in putting your lessons to practice.

- Finally, give a name to the issues that trouble you. For example, let's say that when you feel shy, your hand starts trembling slightly. Name the reaction. Call it jitters and find out how you can stop them. There are things that you can do to keep your hands from jittering uncontrollably.

7

ASK FOR FEEDBACK

*M*ost of us don't like asking for feedback. We are worried about what we might hear. Perhaps we might realize that we were acting strange. Maybe we didn't react in the right way. Or worse, we might have actually offended someone!

No one likes to know that they were acting strange, that they made someone feel bad, or that they were not confident.

One of the big events that I was part of was "Vetrepreneur Day," hosted at the Inc. 500 | 5000 conference. Guess who was the speaker before me? Simon Sinek. Yes, THE Simon Sinek. I thought I had done a pretty good job with my content. But I wanted to receive genuine feedback. I didn't want to just rely on my self-observation. And so, I spoke to Inc.'s editor-in-chief, Eric Schurenberg, and asked him for his opinion. The thing about Eric is that he is a straight shooter. He says it like it is. His response was this: "Well, it just wasn't that good. It wasn't polished."

Now I had two options before me. Let me tell you what I was going through: I was devastated. There was a sense of genuine disappointment coursing through me. Despite what I felt, I could:

- Scoff at Eric's feedback, thinking that no one can understand the effort that I put into the presentation. I am good. It's just that people are either envious, or they are just being picky for the sake of being picky.
- Take the feedback I was given and improve myself. I could be better. And then, I can reach a position where people are genuinely going to enjoy my presentation.

I chose the latter. Why? Because I wasn't about to ignore feedback that could help me improve. Too many people in the world offer empty platitudes.

Not many tell you what you can do to improve or offer honest and constructive criticism.

So why is feedback important? For a whole list of reasons.

Actually listening to feedback and working on your skills is a rewarding process. In fact, the more you train yourself to understand feedback instead of reacting to it immediately, the more you train your mind to become stronger. You slowly eliminate shyness and build a shield of confidence. People won't be able to intimidate you anymore. You will be emboldened to try out new things in life. After all, if you are not doing it right, you are open to someone telling you about it.

When you get used to listening to feedback, you are also creating better connections with people. Do note that not everyone in the world who offers criticism is a horrible person. Some of them are genuinely giving you an opportunity to improve. So why not take the opportunity to show them that you appreciate their comments? In fact, I have made powerful connections with VIPs and influential people because I was willing to listen to them and show them how much I appreciated the fact that they were willing to help me improve.

But in the end, it is all about you.

You see, perhaps you are a good critic when it comes to yourself. Your ability to gauge your mistakes and then provide the right solutions may be absolutely legendary in scope. You might be able to carefully scrutinize every aspect of your personality and point out the flaws. Or on the other hand, maybe you are not comfortable evaluating yourself, which in my opinion is nothing to be ashamed of. I wasn't someone who could look at myself and tell with absolute certainty what was going on in my communication abilities and my personality.

However, whether you are exemplary at self-evaluation or not, there is nothing like feedback to set you on the right path.

When I was in high school, I had a professor who was known for giving honest feedback and helping people better themselves. The problem was that not many were willing to listen to him because of the fact that he was a perfectionist. I so happened to be in his class and he would listen to my presentations and tell me, "I don't think you are bold enough. It seems as though you are holding yourself back."

I decided to take his advice to heart and started working on my stage presentation skills. Soon, I was able to stand in front of a large audience and present my topic without stumbling through my words a lot or feeling too nervous that it would cripple me. Yet my professor's comment was, "I still don't think you are bold enough."

I was frustrated. What was I doing wrong? I had improved so much that others would come to me and compliment my presentation skills. Despite all of that, the professor seemed like he was looking at a work-in-progress that wasn't making the progress he was yearning to see. Eventually, I decided to ask him directly the meaning of his words.

I would never forget the response he gave me.

He looked at me and with sincerity in the eyes said, "I was wondering when you would ask me. You see, it is not the *way* you present, but *what* you present. You talk about interesting topics that have so many areas to cover. Yet, your content seems so mellow. You are not making any impact with your presentations. What you are doing is playing safe."

He then went on to tell me that I could do one of two things.

- I could play it safe and use content that would not challenge people's ideas. That way, I won't be able to create an impact, but I will be able to please more people.
- On the other hand, I could challenge

people's perceptions, be bold and
approach topics that others would not. I
would not be able to please a lot of
people. But I would be able to make deep
impacts.

He told me that ultimately, the choice was up to me.

I took the second option and I am glad that I did. You see, as I had mentioned earlier, the world is going to judge you no matter what you do or say. I can say with certainty that you can be the most generous person and the world will still find ways to point out flaws.

Let me give you an example.

Jeff Bezos once donated nearly $100 million to charity. Many people commended his actions, yet there were those who talked about how small the amount of donation was as compared to his wealth. They said that if he truly wanted to make a difference, he should have donated more than that. How about $500 million? Maybe even a billion perhaps? That would have been something.

Yet those very same people failed to see the $100 million that he donated. When I think about it, I think about the fact that there was $100 million in a particular institution that could be used for good. There was $100 million when before, there wasn't even a tenth of that amount. Whether you donate $10 or a million, you have made a difference. Why? Because that $10 wasn't there before. Now it is. It can be used.

Others talked about the fact that Jeff Bezos merely donated for publicity. Well, I would like to pose this question; even if he did it for publicity, he donated a large amount. What about those with good intentions? How much did they donate?

I am not saying that good intentions are bad. Absolutely not. In fact, I have been talking about kindness and compassion throughout this book. However, when it comes to charity and donations, merely showing good intentions is not going to make a difference.

People are going to judge you. There is no stopping that. But you decide what you want to do about it.

However, that presents a problem doesn't it? I just told you to listen to criticism, but I am also telling you to not pay attention to what people have to say. So what is it?

And here, I would like to present something that I call *Developmental Feedback.*

There are two parts that you need to be aware of.

THE FEEDBACK MODULE

In this part, you are going to learn how to take feedback and find out what you should be listening to and what you should censor out.

Let me give you four sentences and after reading them, I would like you to stop reading any further and mentally decide which of the sentences were feedback, and which weren't. Ready?

- "Awesome job on the task, Jonathan."
- "I would recommend that next time, you make your points more clear Sarah."
- "If your visuals were more related to the subject, then you would have delivered a clear message."
- "Think about your body language and then work through them until you are confident about them."

Pause here. Do not read any further.

Do not worry about giving the right or wrong answer. Imagine someone provides you with the above responses. How would you react? Would you think of them as feedback?

Have you completed categorizing the sentences? Well, then let me present you with the answer.

The truth is, none of them are feedback.

Most of the sentences above are either compliments or advice. And the truth about advice is that it does not always equate to genuine feedback. Advice is not specific enough to be actionable. And that presents a problem to you since you still don't know what to do with that advice.

The four sentences above do not give you pointers on how to improve. They are not descriptive and they aren't making it clear what you have to do.

Let's take the third sentence for example:

"If your visuals were more related to the subject, then you would have delivered a clear message."

Well, what visuals is the person talking about? If you had presented a whole set of visuals, then which of them would you need to remove and which were actually good? And then comes the question of relatability; what ideas does the person have in mind that helps you relate visuals to your presentation? Nothing is quite clear, isn't it? You could comb through your presentation, wracking your brain to find out what visual the person was referring to.

None of the sentences have provided any benchmarks or comparisons. If I tell you that you could improve your presentation by trying to check out Gary Vaynerchuk and see if you can practice some of his body language, I am giving you proper feedback. I am telling you what resources you can use. You can check out any Gary Vaynerchuk video and instantly, you will be able to tell what Gary is doing that you are not doing yourself. Now you have a barometer. You can pick some of Gary's actions and incorporate them into your presentation.

Also, don't forget that the timeliness of the feedback is important. If someone provides a list of things that were wrong with your presentation after a truly long time, then is it going to be valuable to you?

Let's put everything we have just learnt into the feedback. Here is what constructive feedback should look like.

"Awesome job on the task, Jonathan. *You addressed the essential topics in great depth, and you made sure to add details that the client may not have otherwise known. I like the fact that you sent the response earlier than expected. It must have pleased the client considerably.*"

"*I liked the introduction that you gave. However, when you launched into the topic, there was a lot of technical information without any background. It made it difficult to understand some of the concepts. Remember in slide three where you talked about a particular concept and then delved deeper into it? That was brilliant.* I would recommend that next time, you make your points more clear, Sarah."

"When you were talking about the subject, it was highly informative and engaging. I even liked the humor you added to the presentation. Unfortunately, there were a few visuals that did not match the content. For example, in slide five, you talked about social media marketing, but the visual showed a billboard. If your visuals were more related to the subject, then you would have delivered a clear message."

"Think about your body language and then work through them until you are confident about them. *When you were talking, it seemed like your hands were almost attached to your body. Try out a few ways to express yourself and then you can think about whether you are comfortable with them."*

Notice the difference? The feedback itself hasn't changed, yet the sentences provide more context and details to help you understand what you are supposed to do. In fact, with the first feedback, you were able to receive a compliment with the exact reason why. Now you can double-down on those things that you did right.

Having someone tell you what you can improve can be valuable. You can automatically adjust your performance, correct aspects of your communication that require changes, and improve yourself in many ways.

Does that mean that every piece of feedback provided to you is wrong, especially if people don't provide any details? That's not entirely true. So what makes feedback appropriate and what makes it inappropriate?

For one, if you aren't looking for feedback and someone gives it to you anyway, then take it with a pinch of salt. Think about the feedback I got from Eric. He didn't just walk over to me and start pestering me with advice. I sought out his opinion, and he gave me an honest response. In fact, back then I wasn't really looking for feedback. Not because I didn't want to, but Eric was an extremely busy person. So without trying to disturb his work, I wanted a quick opinion. On the other hand, if you start receiving unsolicited advice, then try to evaluate if you truly need such advice at that moment. If not, then consider the person giving you advice. Is he or she an expert on the subject matter? Do they have any valuable experience to share?

Not all negative feedback is wrong. If someone tells you that your presentation was horrible or that you are a terrible singer, do not be offended. You know that you haven't been provided constructive criticism, but just one person's opinion. Your next task is to turn that opinion into feedback. Seek out the advice of a professional or an expert in the matter. I would even go so far as to recommend taking the advice of multiple people, if you can. When you have sufficient feedback, you can then start implementing it effectively.

THE CONFIDENCE MODULE

Once you have the right kind of feedback and you are implementing it into your life, it is time to think about judgements and opinions.

When I was through a phase where I was improving my sales skills, I had a really good instructor. He was brutally honest, but he would tell you what was wrong and how to improve it. I took his advice and started focusing on those areas that needed work.

When I was working to improve myself, I began

to show results. After a while, I noticed that a few people were talking about my work. When I started reaching my targets, someone told me that I would have not been able to do it if not for the help of my mentor. Another person claimed that I was intentionally given easy potential clients to reach out to.

Of course, I didn't reject any claims immediately. I even asked to transfer some of the clients that I had to someone else and took up rather challenging prospects.

I got the same results.

When you are genuinely putting effort into what you do or you make a change in your own way, then you are bound to receive criticism. People can be critical about practically anything that they come across. But that does not always equate to constructive feedback.

Let's take the example of Jeff Bezos.

- Did he donate money? Yes.
- Was it a lot of money? Nobody can deny it was.
- Can it make a difference? Absolutely!

Then he does not have to listen to anyone criticizing him.

I am going to take my example right here.

- Did I practice and improve myself? I did.
- Was I able to show better results because of my improvements? Absolutely.
- Did I become a better salesperson? I did.

There is always a difference between constructive and unsolicited and negative criticism. When people are not supportive of your growth, you might become the target of some rather scathing remarks. Do not simply listen to hurtful comments because you think that they are going to hold a nugget of information. There are plenty of ways to get feedback, and listening to someone berate or insult you is not one of them.

Never listen to someone who smiles to your face and then goes behind your back to say something negative about you. When criticism is constructive, the person will come to you to talk about it. They want to see you improve, so their actions are genuine and heartfelt.

Finally, if someone goes on to social media and posts about your progress or performance under the guise of feedback, don't take their words seriously. Why? Well, let me ask you this:

- Did you explicitly give them permission to broadcast about you?
- Were you looking for their advice on social media, and even if you were, was your intention to chat with them privately or read their feedback displayed to all their friends?

If your answer to the above questions were no, then you don't have to think about whether the person's reactions were truly feedback or not.

SPEAK MORE TO CONNECT MORE

The ability to speak with confidence and express yourself well is an important skill. You are going to better connect with people if you are able to speak to them confidently and with a genuine will to connect. I got to meet the president of Bank of America Merrill Lynch. We bonded over a wonderful conversation. We have since become such good friends that we are godparents to each other's children. To be candid with you, I don't think I would have been able to connect with such an important person with the attitude and approach to conversations I had when I was a bit younger.

Learn to take feedback. But also learn to differentiate between feedback and unwanted criticism.

When you do, listen to feedback and turn your back to all the unnecessary hate and prejudice thrown your way; they are not going to serve any purpose other than bring you down.

8

PRACTICE MINDFULNESS

When one of my close friends first mentioned mindfulness to me, I just tuned him out immediately. I wasn't going to fall for some "get your mind in the right place through meditation and yoga" crap. I was not interested, and at that time I thought I would never change my mind about mindfulness.

How wrong I was.

I eventually understood that I was jumping to conclusions too quickly. I hadn't even tried yoga or meditation, and there I was, making up my mind about them. The only real way to see if I was not into the whole mindfulness idea was to put it into practice.

And so, I started with a simple meditation exercise. The results were good. To be fair, I didn't just try it for a day and then called it quits. That would not have been considered a proper evaluation. I meditated for about two weeks, making sure that I stuck to a strict timetable. I even used a technique that would involve at least 30 minutes of mindfulness. I could have chosen a simple 5-minute meditation, but that would not have allowed me to properly evaluate whether meditation was good for me or not. And let's face it, the conclusion that I would have drawn after short meditation sessions might have been rather biased. I needed to properly see if meditation could have a positive effect on me.

Two months later, I was still meditating, and my sessions had extended to nearly 45 minutes. I was feeling a sense of serenity and calm that I had never experienced before. More importantly, I was able to dispel negative thoughts from my head easily.

Now I am not saying that five-minute meditation sessions are not useful. Hardly. Dan Harris, co-anchor of Good Morning America and Nightline, once mentioned in a Forbes article that he was able to remove negative thoughts from his mind by meditating for just five minutes a day. And you can do that too.

In fact, here is a five-minute meditation technique that you can use whether you are on a busy subway or bus, in an office, or in your home.

If you can find a quiet place, that's great. But if you are on a subway or bus, and it is fairly crowded, don't worry about it. You can still perform the meditation, albeit with different results.

You can choose to close your eyes if the situation allows for it, or you can focus on a particular point. Think about what is more convenient for you. I would also recommend waiting until you come to your stop on the subway or bus before you start your meditation, so that you can clear your mind better and not worry about missing your stop, but if you feel the need to use meditation in order to calm your mind, feel free to use it anywhere you are able to.

- Take in a few deep breaths. Allow the air to enter your lungs and feel it fill up your abdomen. Don't worry about anything. Just focus on the breaths.
- Now bring your breath to a gentle rhythm. Just don't worry about how deep you are breathing. Just keep your breaths steady.
- Start by taking a breath in while slowly counting to five. Try to take your breath

into your abdomen area. Feel that area expand and fill up with air.

- Hold your breath as you count to four.
- Then exhale your breath as you count to five.
- Keep repeating the above steps.

Depending on what's on your mind, the challenges you are facing in life, or the amount of stress you are trying to manage, you are going to find that your mind conjures random thoughts. Some of these thoughts are pleasant ideas, while others may be rather uncomfortable memories. What I want you to do when you find yourself thinking about such negative thoughts – essentially thoughts, ideas, and memories that make you uncomfortable, scared, upset, sad, or create other negative emotions – is not to ignore them. Instead, make a note of them, give them a label, and then move on. For example, let's say that a rather uncomfortable memory from your past crossed your mind. Simply note it as "Memory - Uncomfortable" and then move on.

If the thought is fairly stubborn and refuses to go away, don't try to force it out of your mind. Don't even try to acknowledge it or understand it. Simply repeat the above step. Label it as "Memory - Uncomfortable" and then move on.

Let's say that another idea comes into your head that makes you feel sad, then simply label it as "Idea - Sad" and then move on.

Remember that it does not matter what you label your thoughts. They can be ideas or memories. In fact, all your thoughts can all be labelled as ideas if you like, just so you are not struggling to name them.

When it comes to emotions, I simply like to use the word "uncomfortable." I don't have to struggle with defining the emotions I am going through. You can pick one word for all the emotions you go through or categorize them separately. It is entirely up to you.

- Continue breathing as you push away your thoughts. Keep breathing for about five minutes.

Here are a few things that you should know about this meditation technique:

- You are not going to be able to easily push away the thoughts when you first start to meditate, but as you keep practicing the technique, you will be able to clear your mind much easily.

- You will be able to reap the benefits of meditation on the first attempt. You are going to feel much calmer and you will be able to quieten your raging mind, even slightly.
- The five-minute meditation also teaches you how to master your thoughts. You can use the lessons learnt from meditation in your everyday life.
- I highly recommend that when you start practicing meditation, you set aside a specific time every day. However, I understand that it might not always be possible for you to meditate at the same time every single day.

If you would like to know more about meditation, you can refer to a truly helpful article for beginners published by Jack Canfield. It is called *How to Meditate for Clarity, Intuition, and Guidance* and it truly gives you some wonderful insights into meditation and a step-by-step instructions guide. Plus, it's free!

DAILY ACTIVITIES

When you are having a rough day or you have a lot on your mind, it helps to anchor your thoughts on things that you are familiar with. Ideally, these things should be activities that improve something in your life. For example, making your bed every morning and then starting off your day with a glass of water are examples of simple daily things that lead to an improvement. Making the bed obviously keeps your bedroom more tidy and drinking water is healthy for you.

But how do these things help us? Welcome to the world of priming.

Our subconscious mind is powerful. Any idea that we fill it with becomes embedded in our memories. Though we may not know whether that idea still exists, our subconscious mind has access to it. The reason you like rock music or muscle cars may have roots in your childhood, but often, your tastes and preferences manifest themselves automatically. For example, over the years you might have gotten used to different kinds of music, but for some reason you find yourself still mostly drawn to rock music. It's not a conscious decision that you make every day. It just happens that when you are browsing through

YouTube or checking out playlists on Spotify, you tend to favor rock music.

That's priming taking place on a grand scale. On a much smaller scale, it happens to you every day. The argument with your boss may put you in a foul mood and you might think you have calmed yourself, only to react strongly to a minor situation later during the day. A little sad music may put you in a sombre mood for the rest of the day without you even realizing it.

Priming affects you in numerous ways, which is why you can use it to your advantage. You might have noticed people reading motivational quotes or videos in the morning. You might have scoffed at their attempts to feel good, thinking that such quotes or videos won't really have any effect. But they do.

When you start doing something positive, you keep that positivity in your mind. Later, when you are faced with a challenging situation, your positivity helps you create positive solutions.

Unless your job absolutely requires it – for example, you are a journalist or a reporter – do not watch or read bad news early in the morning. Start the day with something more positive: think about preparing a nice breakfast for yourself, exercise at home or head to the gym, take a walk or go jogging. These ideas may sound rather small, but the point is that you are accomplishing something first thing in the morning.

Whether you successfully exercise or prepare a good breakfast for yourself, that is your first win for the day. You have accomplished something; that in turn gives you a boost to tackle other tasks for the rest of the day.

But what do you do when you are overwhelmed by stress or a panic attack? Perhaps you are about to give a really big presentation or deliver an important message. You are unable to find the right words. It feels as though you are a nervous wreck. You are unsure if you will even be able to complete the task. As it stands, you might as well give up, pack your bags, and go home.

Not so fast.

Understand what is happening to you. Your body has detected a threat in the environment. The threat is the presentation or the act of conveying the message. At that point, your fight-or-flight instincts are overpowering your mind. All the necessary chemicals and hormones are released in your body.

Essentially, it feels as though your body is going to war when in fact, the threat is not in the external world, but in the internal one. I am referring to your mind.

You might experience sweaty palms, faster heart rate, or shallow breathing; they can all be managed if you simply follow a few tips.

Firstly, stop reacting. Break free from the area of stress. For example, step out or distance yourself from a particular person or object. You can even ask for some time to think or plan for the situation. Take 10 to 20 minutes alone.

Then meditate using the five-minute technique I have discussed above. The meditation technique will allow you to see what kind of thoughts are in your mind and try to remove them.

Your colleagues or people around you might find it odd that you took a short break, it is a far better alternative than losing your cool in front of them. In fact, when you return after the break and deal with the situation better, people won't even remember the fact that you have taken a break. Their minds are occupied with the memory of you dealing with the situation properly.

I would also like to point out another important psychological phenomenon that can take place in the event of a fight-or-flight situation: freezing. If you suddenly feel "drained" or start losing interest in what you need to do, especially following a stressful situation, then do note that you are entering the "freeze" state. I would like you to be aware of this reaction and if you notice it, do not panic. Simply take a 10- or 20-minute break and then meditate. Clear your head of any stray thoughts or ideas, so that you are able to think rationally.

LOVING KINDNESS

As human beings, we are all a collection of experiences. What you may have experienced in your life may not be the same as what I may have experienced in mine; that means that you have a different view than me or your friend. There is a certain lens that you look through, and it may not always be rose-colored.

However, despite our experiences and the fact that we react to situations differently, it is important for us to practice kindness.

The kinder you are, the better you are able to practice empathy. You are able to understand people better and reserve less judgement for them. All of these changes help you genuinely connect with people, but you are not going to be able to do it if you are not willing to be kind and understand the other person.

I believe in the notion that you need to give

respect in order to receive it. You cannot automatically expect people to hand it over to you: that is called entitlement and it is a truly destructive frame of mind to have.

Start showing kindness. Take the initiative to give respect, but do not expect anything in return. Here's why:

- If people understand your kindness and respond to you in kind, then you know that you have found a person you can form genuine connections with.
- If you notice people ignoring your kindness and respect, or disrespecting you for no apparent reason, you know who to avoid as much as possible.

You can truly see a person's character when you show respect to them and see their response.

What happens if people do not respond to the respect you show them? Common wisdom might suggest that you ignore those people entirely. I would like you to do otherwise. Do not ignore people who don't show you the same level of respect you show them. After all, they could become important contacts who might be able to help you in the future.

However, do not spend too much time with them, especially if you are working at improving your charisma. You could instead spend your time with people who respond to your respect positively. They can help you boost your communication skills and your overall charisma.

I will take this tip one step further and say: speak with intent. Don't just say the first thing that comes to your mind. Think about it for a while and then, if you think it is appropriate for the situation, speak in a calm and confident manner.

Here is something you should know. When we don't filter our thoughts, we are more likely to say something embarrassing. And the more embarrassing or awkward situations we find ourselves in, the more we stop believing that we have any semblance of charisma.

Take your time to think about what you would like to say. While thinking, remember to:

- Be generous in your praise, but only when it is deserved.
- Explain your feelings clearly, confidently, and more importantly, accurately.
- Listen intently. Don't start using your

phone or getting distracted when
someone is talking to you.

SILENCE BEFORE MEETINGS

You don't have to launch into a verbal barrage of information as soon as your meetings start. A few seconds of silence will allow everyone in the room to settle down, and they will be able to organize their thoughts. When you allow people in the room to get a good head start, they will maintain a positive momentum throughout the meeting. If, on the other hand, you start off hurriedly and not allow people to get a good start, the entire meeting is going to be a compilation of nervousness, hesitation, perhaps even awkwardness.

I would even go one step further and conduct the meeting – whenever possible of course – without the use of smartphones or laptops. Send across an invite a few days in advance detailing the topics that will be handled during the meeting. When people are in the room, make sure that you allow genuine human interactions not bogged down by devices.

EMAIL RESPONSIBLY

When you practice mindfulness, you are able to better analyze the world around you: when it comes to emails, you are able to read them clearly. If you feel your mind populated with numerous thoughts, take a moment to calm your thoughts. Read through the email. Take a few seconds to let the message sink into your mind, then read the email again.

When responding to the email, make sure you put yourself in the shoes of the other person. Sometimes it's tempting to respond with sarcasm or a powerfully scathing remark. But what is that going to do, other than satisfy a petty sense of payback? Wouldn't you rather clear off misunderstandings and forge better relationships? Additionally, if you were the recipient of the message, would you like reading what you just typed?

I would also recommend not checking your emails each time you received a notification. Allot a time for emails and only check them during that allotted time. For example, you may not want to be bothered during the weekends. Take care of all your emails before the start of the weekend, so that you can take that time for yourself.

CONCLUSION

As you finish this book, I want you to know one thing: nothing is going to happen instantaneously. I mention this because too often, people fail to see instant results and they are overcome with disappointments. They feel that they are not capable of changing, or that a charismatic lifestyle isn't for them.

That's not true. Think about the fact that every habit you have right now has developed over a period of years. You have spent a considerable amount of time building yourself into the person you are today. You cannot expect to completely eradicate years of effort and experiences in a matter of days or weeks.

Keep practicing the tips and techniques mentioned in this book. Usually, after a period of around 30 days, you will be able to spot slight changes. Sometimes, and if you are lucky, the changes may be drastic. But whether those changes are big or small, they are all a sign of improvement.

The road to charisma improvement is paved with gradual growth and development. Do not become frustrated easily: all your hard work is going to pay off in the end, and you will become a more charismatic person.

ABOUT THE AUTHOR

John Ward is a professor, a motivational speaker, an author, and holds two degrees in psychology and neuroscience. He has devoted his life to helping people become their best selves both in the classroom and in countless books.

With his background in behavioral sciences and developmental psychology, John has managed to help numerous people overcome their self-defeating habits in order to become better individuals. He has been a star speaker at self-improvement conferences, local centers for the underprivileged, and sometimes even at college graduations. John wishes to help as many people transform their lives for the better before he himself turns fifty years old.

When he's not writing or teaching, John enjoys traveling the world with his adoring wife of almost twenty years by his side. And because John is a family man, first and foremost, he enjoys spending the free time that he has, with his family. He is proud to father two amazing and successful sons, one of whom, wishes to follow in his father's footsteps and become a motivational speaker himself.

REFERENCES

Carnegie, D. (2007). *How to win friends & influence people*. New York: Pocket Books.

Cohen, S. (2006). *Win the crowd*. William Morrow Paperbacks.

Cowan, N. (2010). The Magical Mystery Four. Current Directions In Psychological Science, 19(1), 51-57. doi: 10.1177/0963721409359277

Edwards, V. Priming Psychology: How to Get People to Do What You Want. Retrieved 22 April 2020, from https://www.scienceofpeople.com/priming-psychology/

Keating, S. (2019). The science behind why some of us are shy. https://www.bbc.com/future/article/20190604-the-science-behind-why-some-of-us-are-shy

Murphy, J. (2011). *The power of your subconscious mind.* Mansfield Centre, CT: Martino Pub.

Queensland Government. (2016). Communicating effectively for business. https://www.business.qld.gov.au/running-business/marketing-sales/managing-relationships/communicating-effectively

Scientific American. (2012). Lingering with a Decision Breeds More Indecision. https://www.scientificamerican.com/podcast/episode/lingering-with-a-decision-breeds-mo-12-07-08/

Printed in Great Britain
by Amazon